W9-AAO-832

hooray!

Book design by Emily Horne of **asofterworld.com**.
Cover design by Emily Horne and Chip Zdarsky. **They're good people.**

Copyright 2010. All rights reserved. No portion of this book may be reproduced or transmitted without express written permission from the copyright holders, except for brief excerpts for review purposes.

Published by **TopatoCo Books**, a division of **The Topato Corporation**.
116 Pleasant St. Ste 203
Easthampton, MA 01027

Dinosaur Comics are available online in a free but much-less-tangible state at **qwantz.com**.
TopatoCo is online at **topatoco.com**.

First Edition, November 2010
ISBN-13: 978-0-9824862-6-9

10 9 8 7 6 5 4 3 2 1

Printed in China

To my sweetie Jenn,

who wasn't around when I wrote these comics,
but WHATEVER

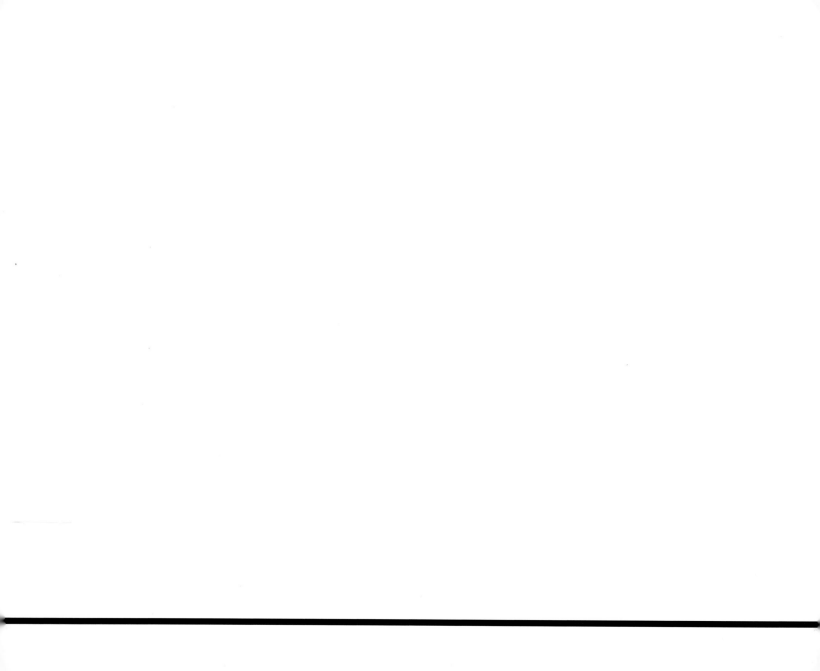

DINOSAUR COMICS:

Dudes Already Know About Chickens
By Ryan North

Introduction

My mom reads just two webcomics – mine (to my occasional embarrassment), and Ryan North's. I get calls from her about him. She says she's calling about something else, but then she finds a way to bring him up. "Ryan North's post today was so funny," she'll say. "He seems like such a nice boy." She's clearly stopping herself just short of saying, "why can't you be more like him?" And I can't blame her. I love Ryan's comics, too, and have for many years.

The world is changing. Over the past few decades, the written word, previously a vessel for printed instructions, literature, and the occasional long letter, has increasingly become a tool for minute-to-minute casual communication. Ryan, perhaps thanks to to his background in computational linguistics, has proven himself a master of conveying a friendly, happy-go-lucky conversational tone in every part of his writing. His skill shows in his deployment of punctuation, typefaces, caps lock, and odd phrase structures that appear to have been architected by a friendly surfer dude with a magnetic poetry set containing every word in the language. Every choice is made carefully and precisely – not to show off his skill, like some writers might, but simply to create that perfect congenial vibe that makes readers around the world feel that if they met him, they'd get along fabulously.

The format of Dinosaur Comics suggests some obvious questions: if the panels never change, does it really count as a comic? If so, is it just variations on one comic, or many? Is it really art at all?

I think the best thing about these questions is that I hardly ever hear them anymore. Ryan North has published year after year of creative, funny Dinosaur Comics, neither repeating himself nor resorting to increasingly desperate gimmicks as a source of novelty. And over the years, people seem to have lost interest in figuring out what they should or shouldn't say about his work, probably because it's so much more fun and satisfying to just *read* it.

But I think the biggest reason for Dinosaur Comics's continued success is that it is, more than anything else, an ongoing conversation about how strange, fascinating, and just plain cool the world is. You hold a piece of that conversation in your hands, and the world it loves is all around you. So cheer up! You've made a friend.

— RANDALL MUNROE

Randall Munroe is the creator of xkcd.com.

EINSTEIN PREDICTED THE EXISTENCE OF ANTI-DOLLARS IN A LITTLE-KNOWN PAPER IN 1945!
IT WAS OVERSHADOWED BY ATOMIC BOMB FEVER

LOGICAL FALLACY COMICS
today's fallacy:
BEGGING THE QUESTION

Begging the question is when what you're trying to prove is assumed implicitly in one of your premises!

FOR EXAMPLE: T-Rex is a pretty sweet dude because he's always so friggin' awesome!

This is actually formally valid: if the premise is true and I'm friggin' awesome, then it follows that I'm a pretty sweet dude. However, I've provided no logical support for my "T-Rex is awesome" premise, but only made a conclusion (T-Rex = pretty sweet) which relies on the premise being true. I haven't offered any evidence, so I am begging the question!

But "begging the question" is mostly used today to mean "raising the question"!

I know! IT'S SO WRONG.

Well, I suppose that begs the question, T-Rex: if it's used more often to mean "raises the question" than "a fallacy of presumption", doesn't that suggest that the definition of the phrase has evolved?

NO IT DOES NOT. What it suggests is that everybody sucks but me!

LATER: THE FACE OF PRESCRIPTIVE LANGUAGE??

everyone else is all 'oh i felt like i could really make a difference here' and t-rex is all 'well, uh, i wanted to show up my friend? he's a utahraptor'

later: CLEARLY reluctant double high fives

the implication here is that 'green' does rhyme with 'machine' and that t-rex calls himself 'the green machine' OKAY

Is it possible to have adventures in today's modern world? I mean real adventures, like ones where I get to swashbuckle.

T-Rex says, "probably not!"

I think we've made our environment so predictable and safe that there's no real opportunity to go where nobody's been before, to see things that haven't been seen. It's too bad! I want ADVENTURES.

What about things like EXTREME SNOWBOARDING?

While clearly extreme, can such activities truly be considered capital-A Adventure?

Sure they can, T-Rex! You see new things, and there's danger.

I don't know...

Man, some dudes are EXTREME!! enough to snowboard down Mount Everest! There's a real chance you could be killed doing that, PLUS, only a few people have ever done it. I'd call that "adventure"!

Especially since you'd have to climb up at least part of Everest yourself. Okay, you're right!

MEANWHILE, IN THE UNIVERSE WHERE EVERYONE SNOWBOARDS EVERYWHERE:

Guys, I REALLY just don't think I'm as into snowboarding as I used to be.

698

there's a cut panel where the devil talks about a time when one of his atari games burnt out while he was playing it, and how the resulting smoke was the smell of adventure

really, it's unfair that utahraptor's plan didn't work, because more wishes is a very reasonable thing to ask for. a lot of problems could be solved with more wishes.

IT'S NOT ACTUALLY THAT ATTRACTIVE BUT EVERYONE SAYS IT IS BECAUSE OF COLONIALISM

if you are a dude who thinks puberty actually is a nightmare, then sorry for reminding you :(

It occurs to me that democracy is pretty unfair if you're not a dude who's in the majority!

DEMOCRACY COMICS

It sucks, because if everyone disagrees with you, then you'll never get anything you want. It's majority rule! MOB rule!

Well, majority rule is sort of the definition of democracy, T-Rex. Not everyone can get everything they want!

Yeah, but what if the majority decided to be totally racist against you? You're pooched!

People have worried about this before, my friend!

What do they say?

Well, what you're worried about is called the "tyranny of the majority", and it's usually countered by the observation that there's at least a push for minority rights being respected in a democracy, since we're all minorities in one way or another.

Right! Like how I'm in a minority because I sometimes like to sleep in on weekends.

Actually, I'd say most people like to do that, T-Rex.

Really? Are you serious??

Have all my years of sleepy shame been for naught?

blinking in the afternoon sunlight, already fabricating the first lies of morning productivity

703

Vegetarians are chicks and dudes who don't eat a lot of meat for some reason or whatever!

DIFFERENT TYPES OF VEGETARIANISM

First off, you've got your lacto-ovo vegetarians, who don't eat meat but do eat eggs and milk. There's also lacto vegetarians and ovo vegetarians. Then you've got your vegans, who don't eat meat or ANY animal products, so eggs, honey, milk, and cheese are out, and even leather sometimes. For - for shoes.

And pants?

My favourite are the freegans!

Where you be vegetarian for free?

Close! It's where you don't eat meat unless you're given it for free, like from a dumpster. You prevent meat from going to waste, but you don't support its production.

That sounds close to flexitarians, who only eat meat when being vegetar-ian would be rude or inconvenient!

Now, I myself am a tremendo-meatatarian, which means that I only eat meat that I find to be tremendously delicious!

I've seen you eat fruits and vegetables!

Yes. On account of the golly gosh-darned scurvy.

704

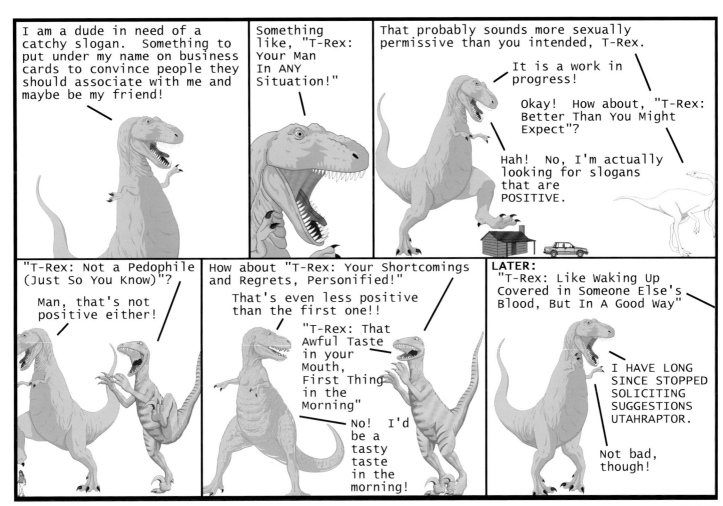

My old hometown of Ottawa spent $200,000 on a new slogan for the city, and the best they could come up with was 'Technically beautiful'. It was very embarassing to us all. I think the guy who suggested the slogan got a new bike, if memory serves.

705

The city was dark - too dark. The kind of dark that could drive a man insane.

As I parked my retro car outside of my detective agency, I felt for the cool weight of my gun!

Not just cool temperature-wise, but cool in that it made me look good. Too good. But I had to look good, because my first case of the day was my ex-wife, Fran. Turns out she was bein' blackmailed. Couldn't say by who, but I had a pretty good idea of who it might be. The night was turning out to be a real night... to remember.

T-Rex, enough! Is this story supposed to have a case of the sucks?

No! Of course not!

You're kidding me, right? It's stereotypical, but it's like you're not really sure what the stereotypes are. It reads like a parody where they forgot to put in any jokes! Also, is it night or day in the story?

Whoah, ouch! Last time I narrate any of my stories for you, Mr. Critical Pants!

LATER:

Oh right, Utahraptor's having trouble with this dude he's been seeing! I forgive his critical outburst.

"TROUBLE AT HOME?"

706

FUN FACT: Did you know that if you're in a situation where your messages have a chance of being lost or misunderstood, then you can never fully share information with someone?

It's totally true, even if all the messages arrive unmolested!

So Dromiceiomimus, imagine I'm sending you a letter that says "hi". You get it, so now we both know that I said "hi", but only you know that YOU know that I said "hi".

So you send a letter that says "got it", which I get - but then I know that you know that I said "hi", but you don't know that I know that YOU know that I said "hi". And so on!

We go back and forth sending "I got your 'I got it'" letters forever!

So plausible, T-Rex!

Well, of course we wouldn't ACTUALLY do that, but the point is that we can never know the exact same information, unless it's 100% guaranteed that messages aren't lost or garbled. But the mail isn't like this!

Oh man, this is just another one of your dumb postal service conspiracy theories!!

MEANWHILE, IN THE PAST:
I plan on developing SEVERAL crazy theories about the postal service.

to clarify, t-rex plans to theorize that the people responsible for the postal service built their system such that it would take financial advantage of information-theoretic properties of lossy networks :o

for instance, in a book if the main character dies you can't go back and re-read the last few pages over and over again for like two hours trying to get him to survive, before finally throwing the book away in disgust because that last page is friggin impossible

If I were to be reincarnated, I would like it to be as one of those big machines that eats smaller machines for an audience.

T-REX IN: REINCARNATION COMICS

What? They're awesome.

BUT THEN! Does reincarnation work on machines?

What, you're going to shoot down my idea?

No, I've just never heard reincarnation including things that, you know - aren't alive.

Some people believe that you can come back as plants! They're BARELY alive.

They support the entire food chain!

BARELY. So barely! I've seriously never been impressed with a plant.

Even sunflowers? They tilt to follow the sun!

Don't get me started about sunflowers. God! Their salty, boring seeds!

t-rex is not telling the truth. in 1998 he was quite impressed with a flower that bloomed only once a year, and that smelled septic while doing so.

711

Okay, I may have been a little hard on plants. I concede that, yes, there ARE some plants that actually do some cool things.

AN APOLOGY TO PLANTS

FOR EXAMPLE: there's some dogwood plants that have tiny flowers which bloom, explosively, in something like half a millisecond! In doing so, they accelerate their pollen at rocket speeds and blast it out at over four meters per second. That's some fast pollen! And I am not a dude who's gonna say that naturally weaponized flowers aren't cool.

And, I SUPPOSE, plants that cure diseases are pretty alright too.

A retraction!

Well - I realized that I do want plants on my side, even if most of them just sit there. And I do think it's kinda neat how some can turn dirt into strawberries. I've got nothing against strawberries!

You love strawberries.

I do love strawberries.

HOW MUCH DO YOU LOVE STRAWBERRIES T-REX

I don't know. A lot? They're alright.

To - to fully understand my love of strawberries is to fully understand the unblinking eye of madness?

712

t-rex isn't - he isn't quite sure what god wants him to say.

haha yeah there's definitely a stereotypical male fantasy in panel three. women! there's no time for talking about feelings now! we're doing SCIENCE!

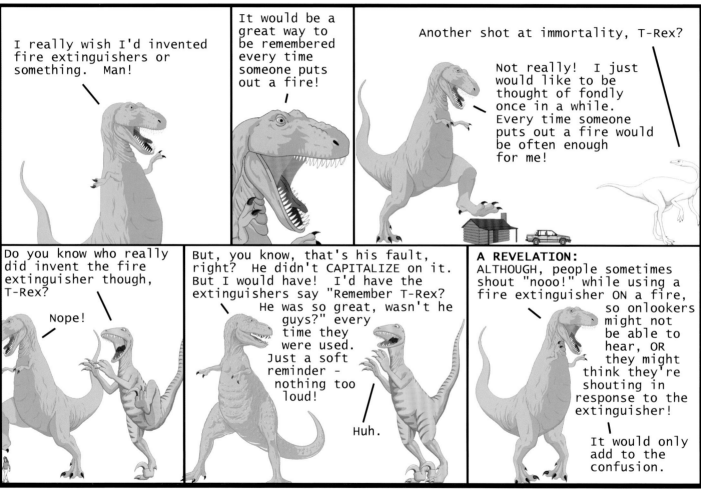

716

SOCIALISM COMICS!

Oh-kay! Socialism is when people share the means of production and stuff. Everyone works together for the common good!

... for some reason!

Haha! See what I did there, Dromiceiomimus? I implied that socialism is flawed because people don't really have a motivation to share with each other.

It's a tragic flaw of our characters that we don't share as often, or as equally, as we should.

Yeah, that - that was my joke.

Making fun of our fundamental flaws, are we? Classy!

Hey!

Holy, why is everyone so touchy about the tragic and fundamental flaws of their nature today? I'm sorry we all don't share enough, but I'm not going to IGNORE it and hope it goes away. I deal with the issues!

Not hardly! You can't deal with the "issue" of socialism by just summing it up in a few sentences!

True! But I can sum it up in a play involving everyone wanting some of my delicious ice cream cone!

What?

And then we all decide to pitch in and take over the ice cream cone factory?

i'm pretty sure that's how it works?

VALENTINE'S DAY EVE:

Okay, this time for sure! I will avoid any troubles on Valentine's Day by simply IGNORING IT. I will deny this manufactured holiday its very existence!

Have I, perhaps, solved the "Valentine's Day Problem" once and for all?

Aww! That's kind of sad, T-Rex. What if someone gives you a so-bad-they're-good valentine, like those little ones with pictures of cars that say things like "I wheelie like you"? Would you really want to turn those down?

Huh! I actually hadn't considered ironic valentines, which I do like. Hmm...

And what if someone wants you to be their valentine for real?

Well...!

Seriously! What happens if a gorgeous, intelligent, funny woman asks you to be her valentine tomorrow? Are you going to shoot her down because you're denying that Valentine's Day exists?

My friend, I will handle that situation by simply "ignoring my principles" and "reversing my position".

ANYWAY, T-REX ENDS UP SPENDING VALENTINE'S DAY ALONE:

Why do they call it "lactose intolerant"? They should call it, "lactose inconsiderate".

the 'Valentine's Day Problem' t-rex is referring to is the problem of what if nobody gives you any valentines!

A singularity refers to a future moment when we create artificial intelligences that are smarter than we are. It's called this because things will be so different, it's impossible to predict past it. Everything will change!

For instance: these smart machines could make even smarter machines!

And so on until we have super duper smart machines that will look on us as mere playthings. Will they destroy us? Or will we merge ourselves with technology, and in doing so become a new, more cybernetic lifeform? Our choices seem limited to either becoming something new, or facing irrelevance and obsolescence!

So why does a super intelligent AI make predictions impossible?

Because too much has changed!

Also because we're too dumb. It'd be like a dog trying to predict what its owner does.

I think most dogs can do that with some accuracy, T-Rex.

Right. Well - I've never really been one for "apt analogies".

T-REX IS TELLING THE TRUTH:

Check it! Eating food in bed is like - a crappy duck?

What the heck, everyone?

is there a message in my doing a comic about 'singularity' on valentine's day? that seems like a bit of a stretch! you are probably overthinking things.

an alternate last line has the devil saying t-rex T-REX MY FAVOURED FOES ARE THE STERN AND IMPLACABLE COLOURED BOXES OF THE BREAKOUT GENRE and then adding OUR PATHS WILL CROSS AGAIN

I would never want to get pregnant. Having to worry about what I eat because there's a baby GROWING inside me? No thanks!

"A MALE PERSPECTIVE"

There's nothing bad about that, T-Rex! It's a special experience and you could probably stand to eat better anyway!

The cravings would be a good excuse for eating all the damn bread, but still! Too much RESPONSIBILITY. I'm dangerously carefree!

Why are we talking about this?

No reason, just - sharing!

Well as none of us can get pregnant because, oh hey, we're not female mammals, it's not something I'd expect you to worry about! "I'd never want to be a dividing cell, because there'd be two of me and we'd be tiny." -T-Rex.

I don't recall saying that!!

LATER:
"I have smelly pants." -Utahraptor.

"I love the taste of chocochops!" -T-Rex?

Man! They are moulded chocolate pork chops with a real pork chop bone. Am I now to apologize for BRILLIANCE?

it's like chocolate combined with the bones of a dead animal? my friend Patrick invented chocochops in real life a few years ago, and if you want to produce chocochops on a large scale, you should really be talking to Patrick.

721

People are sad sometimes, and that makes me very sad. Therefore, I will dedicate my memorable "problem solving skills" towards solving the problem of sadness once and for all!

WAYS TO BE HAPPY

Way to be happy #1: amnesia! Forget your problems!

This has the problem of robbing you of your present, history, and self, however. Most people like those things! So Method #2 is using happiness-inducing DRUGS and ALCOHOL.

That seems to have many of the same limitations as Method #1!

TRUE. But I have other methods! Method #3 is having a rewarding and satisfying professional and personal life. Tada!

But that's more a definition of happiness than a guide to achieving it, T-Rex!

OKAY.

Luckily, I still have Method #4, which is to set unreasonably low expectations for everyone, including yourself.

THAT only works if you're euphoric whenever expectations are met.

MAN! EVERYONE is making it really hard for me to solve the eternal problem of unhappiness!

BUT THEN, INSPIRATION! A PERFECT SOLUTION FOR ENDLESS JOY!

W-...

Wildly misinterpret your own despair?

722

t-rex got a positive mention of his 'problem-solving skills' on his grade three report card, and NEVER FORGOT

Hey, God, would you still hang out with me if I didn't have any friends?

HAHA NOPE

WHAT IF I HAD NO FRIENDS COMICS

starring t-rex the dinosaur

I'm serious! I figure it's harder to make that first friend than it is to make the 20th, and I'm concerned that if I moved to a new town where I didn't know anybody, I wouldn't have any friends.

You're good at making friends though, T-Rex! You're not shy!

But that's just it - I'm just not shy around FRIENDS! It is a catch 22 in my social life!

Well, how did you make friends the first time?

I don't remember, man!

I must have been two years old or something. But I've used that first friend as a seed to get me all my other friends and now I have this irrational fear that my house of cards will come crashing down around me!

Hah! Looks like you'd better be EXTRA nice to us then!

Wait. Wait - I have the solution! All we have to do is make a legally binding promise to be best friends forever, purely out of fear of being alone!

T- That's attractive, right?

so tempted to put up panel 1 and nothing else

arguably, the best form of spying

727

Hysteria was once thought to originate in the womb ("hystera" is the Greek word for "womb"). This had the nice side-effect of making men immune to it!

A HISTORY OF HYSTERIA

It was thought to be caused by the malfunction, or sometimes just the presence, of the uterus. Women were crazy because their wombs were so wacky! People went as far to suggest that women should not be taught, because enlarging the brain would shrink the womb, making them useless as mothers and even MORE hysterical. Treatment sometimes included genital massage!

You sure know a lot about the history of hysteria, T-Rex!

It's true!

And it's why I never call a woman OR a joke "hysterical". I don't want to be accused of tacitly endorsing historically institutionalized sexism!

Hah! I might accuse you of that just for fun.

AW, MAN!

T-REX DECIDES TO EXCISE THE "HYSTERA" ROOT ENTIRELY FROM HIS VOCABULARY, JUST TO BE SAFE:

So I hear you're having a minuswomb operation?

Excuse me? I'm having a hysterectomy.

Yes! A "uter-b-gone".

A womboval?

T-REX MISSED A TRAIN THIS MORNING:

Man, forget that! Time controls TOO MUCH of our modern lives. I will be the one to fight this creeping chronology by becoming its first true antithesis. Yes! I will become...

... the ANTITIME!

Wow, the Antitime, with the full power to reverse time! will you please turn my grandmother into a young woman again?

What? No, I - I don't actually control time. I'm just against the CONCEPT.

So - no taking back mistakes, no solving problems before they ever occur?

Nope!

And why is everyone acting like I can suddenly control time just because I gave myself a sweet superhero name? It's surreal.

Well perhaps the name gave us something to believe in, huh? Perhaps, in the end, the name was greater than the man.

NEXT TIME, ON DINOSAUR COMICS: T-REX WISHES HE ACTUALLY HAD THE POWER TO CONTROL TIME.

Aw frig, my microwave popcorn!!

730

Dear poets, I am sorry I've been making fun of your craft for over 20 years. It is actually harder than it looks!

AN APOLOGY TO

POETS

I have been trying, UNSUCCESSFULLY, to write a poem for the past half hour. I am trying to capture the emotion of getting up early in winter, during a heavy snowfall, and going for a walk and coming across a set of traffic lights (the kind that switch automatically) controlling traffic that won't be there for hours. The sense of seeing them as art, of watching them through the snowfall in the crisp dusk of a new day.

So let's hear what you've written so far!

Okay, but I warn you: it is unfinished.

"Once upon a time / Some traffic lights did time / Colours on the snow / Where oh where did they all go?"

Hah hah! That is definitely the worst poem I've heard all day.

Oh yeah? Well, not if I do... THIS!

"Dancing is crazy; fun to do / Would you like to dance? Yes, you!"

That's actually way better than the last one.

Are there cash awards for poetry, do you know?

utahraptor has already heard 117 separate instances of poetry today. he is truly at a loss to explain it.

it was one of those Adventures that you don't really ever tell your diary about

this comic gets a lot funnier if you replace 'fall in love' with 'masturbate' in the first two panels. it's too bad i don't make sex comics! i'd have the first two panels down cold.

T-REX LET'S INVENT AN AGING MACHINE

A what?

A MACHINE THAT MAKES PEOPLE AGE REAL FAST

COME ON

IT'LL RULE

LATER:

Tada! The aging machine is completed!

Dromiceiomimus, what have YOU done today? I'VE just made a machine that makes people age, with God's help!

So what's the symbolism there? Is it called "The Life Machine" or something?

No. No, that would be good but this is actually just a machine that leaks invisible cell-decaying radiation.

Holy cow! Why would you build something like that?

B-Because God told me to?

That's insanely dangerous, T-Rex! Geez!! I'm leaving. I don't want to be around a dude who has a LIFE-DESTROYING-MACHINE nearby.

Man, you're right! What was I thinking? Well, you can REST ASSURED that I'll be taking this up with God at my earliest convenience.

BUT LATER, ALL IS FORGOTTEN:

So yeah! That's why I can never see myself using the word "twincest".

THAT'S FAIR

734

alternate ending: t-rex actually takes it up with god, and asks what the deal is. 'i believe you said this would rule?' he asks, pointedly.

if you are actually in love with t-rex, and also named mark, then panel 6 is the panel for you

friends, i have bad news! the answer is still actually 'no way'!

737

I'm not going to leave what happens to me after I die up to others. What if they put on a weaksauce funeral?

People might equate a weaksauce funeral with a correspondingly weaksauce dude!

Worse, what if they bury me in an UNCOOL part of the graveyard?

Aww, we wouldn't do that, T-Rex! We would bury you with all the cool kids.

Perhaps! But I've decided to solve this problem ONCE AND FOR ALL by arranging my own funeral, plot and gravestone myself. Tada!

This has actually been done before, my friend!

Really?

Yep! It is a growing trend in the "moribund set". People get everything set up in advance! You can even visit your own grave if you want - the expiry date gets filled in when you die.

Spooky!

Not really, since there's nothing buried there yet! It is pure FORESHADOWING.

Huh! It seems less cool, knowing that it's been done before. But I guess I COULD still visit my grave and pretend to be a time traveller who's changed the past! The whole "Noo! I changed the past!" idea. You know?

Like I'm surprised at how sucky a time traveller I am?

738 it's true! i personally know of TWO people who are doing this 'death in advance' thing. the next time you put flowers on a grave, you should check that the person is actually dead! also this advice was probably appropriate even before people started doing this.

EPIPHANY COMICS

Friends are good things to have! They can help you out when you are sad (a psychological benefit), and can lend you money if you need it (an economic benefit)!

It is these positive benefits of having friends that concern me!

I'm pretty sure I like my friends because of the people they are, but what if I'm just kidding myself? What if I really just like them because they're an economic cushion - someone to bail me out, even literally, if I get into trouble?

Well - I mean, you'd do the same thing for us, T-Rex.

Exactly! We hedge our bets by having friends!

There are friendships that go beyond this shared benefit, T-Rex!

How so?

Okay - what about "best friends forever", the people in your life who you'll know will stand by you no matter what?

They are even MORE of an economic benefit! They are get out of jail free cards, people who you can rely on in any situation.

Wait!! My problem's that I'm seeing any positive effect of friendship as income, and thus everyone involved in one as compromised in a conflict of interest. I would only be happy if having friends was awful!

Thanks, rare and brilliant moments of perfect self-awareness!

740

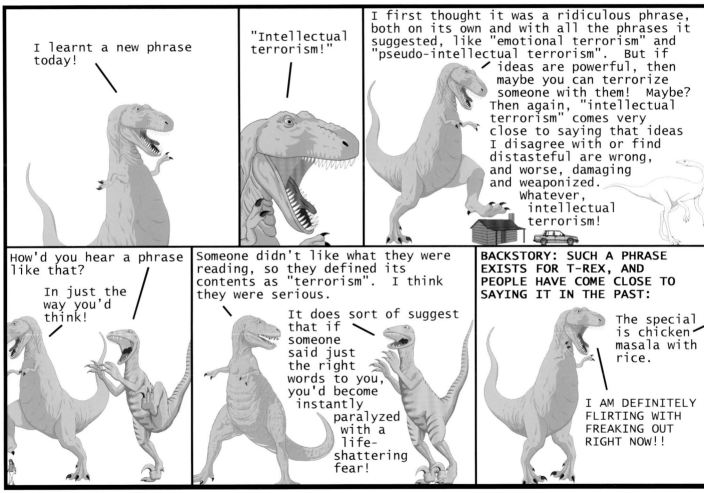

I learnt a new phrase today!

"Intellectual terrorism!"

I first thought it was a ridiculous phrase, both on its own and with all the phrases it suggested, like "emotional terrorism" and "pseudo-intellectual terrorism". But if ideas are powerful, then maybe you can terrorize someone with them! Maybe? Then again, "intellectual terrorism" comes very close to saying that ideas I disagree with or find distasteful are wrong, and worse, damaging and weaponized. Whatever, intellectual terrorism!

How'd you hear a phrase like that?

In just the way you'd think!

Someone didn't like what they were reading, so they defined its contents as "terrorism". I think they were serious.

It does sort of suggest that if someone said just the right words to you, you'd become instantly paralyzed with a life-shattering fear!

BACKSTORY: SUCH A PHRASE EXISTS FOR T-REX, AND PEOPLE HAVE COME CLOSE TO SAYING IT IN THE PAST:

The special is chicken masala with rice.

I AM DEFINITELY FLIRTING WITH FREAKING OUT RIGHT NOW!!

this egg sandwich is breakfast terrorism

741

shout outs to david rees, mnftiu.cc!

alternate ending: t-rex finds an old diary of his while cleaning, flips through it, finds a random entry, and wonders whatever could have compelled him to write the phrase 'brainstorming the castle'. he feels like he'd like to distance himself from his past self.
he sits quietly for a while.

Oh yes, I have an idea for the Best Victimless Prank Ever! Plus it'll give a cashier a good story to tell. Dromiceiomimus, you've got to help me on this one!

Dromiceiomimus?

Dromiceiomimus, there you are!

Here I am!

Dromiceiomimus, I need your help with a prank. The prank is, we all get some really fake stick-on moustaches even though we're all of age, THEN we put them on and go into a convenience store and we all buy ADULT PORNOGRAPHIC MAGAZINES!! Hee hee!

SOON!

Hey, can I get in on this prank too?

Sure can!!

SWEET. I'll come in wearing a moustache after you guys leave, but I'll just buy some milk! That way, the guy at the cash'll be expecting me to hilariously buy some pornos, but no, I'll just buy the milk. Maybe some cheese.

Let's do it!

LATER: A MOMENT OF REFLECTION.

Buying this magazine made me feel dirty and ashamed! Have I once again thoughtlessly aided the exploitation of our nation's topless lesbian teens?

744

arguably, our nation's finest natural resource?

later: batman is so pissed off at the nappy times suggestion that he ACTUALLY BECOMES REAL just to punch the people who have been sniggering!

even the example t-rex gives is fundamentally flawed. who would like to be known as a 'sexual basketball player'? 'sexual basketball' sounds like some game a creepy guy and then try to get you to play with him. what's the deal, creepy guy?

dude's name is 'jacques esqueleto'

747

Hey, have they ever made a video game where you get to control a car and your goal is get it to grow up into a bigger car?

Because they TOTALLY should!

LATER: And so it's like - you need to care for your car to make it grow up into a truck and then an SUV and if you're lucky a monster truck. Maybe a plane. Weird cars grow up into boats.

So it's like a pet, but instead of being cute, it pollutes?

Yes! People are TIRED of animals as pets. They want cars that age! I know because I played a game once and that's what I wanted.

But what's the gameplay mechanic? How does it work?

Dude, I already said!

You take care of little cars and then they grow up into awesome cars or stupid-lookin' boats. The end! Fifty points!

What do you actually DO in the game, though? Do I take my car on nice country drives? Give it drinks of gas and feed it nice oil treats?

"Oil treats"?! Come on! It's called "CHANGING THE OIL", and it gets you a +1 happiness in Car Car Simulator Trucko Boat 3.

Will no-one make my video game dream a fevered reality?

748 the origin of this idea was that t-rex was having a tiff with his dog and wanted to make him EVEN ANGRIER by talking about replacing him with an electronic pet car that ages somehow. then he was like holy cow, how come i'm not playing that game RIGHT NOW??

this comic goes out to all the people with big enough hearts to take in and care for a totally sucky dog

did you notice how i left the gender of the really attractive friend ambiguous? this is so everyone can enjoy their own mental image.
this is because i am a considerate writer who cares about his readers

who among us has not upset the ph balance in our own stomachs as some sort of blind fumble towards entertainment?

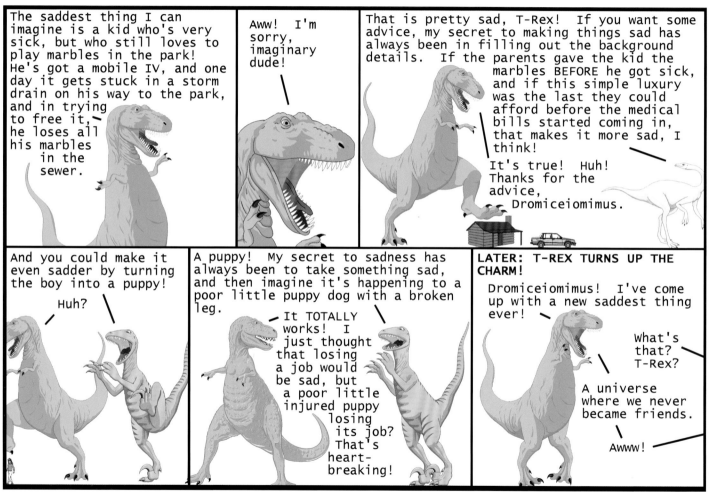

based on a true story :(

The saddest thing I can imagine is a kid who's very sick, but who still loves to play marbles in the park! He's got a mobile IV, and one day it gets stuck in a storm drain on his way to the park, and in trying to free it, he loses all his marbles in the sewer.

Aww! I'm sorry, imaginary dude!

That is pretty sad, T-Rex! If you want some advice, my secret to making things sad has always been in filling out the background details. If the parents gave the kid the marbles BEFORE he got sick, and if this simple luxury was the last they could afford before the medical bills started coming in, that makes it more sad, I think!

It's true! Huh! Thanks for the advice, Dromiceiomimus.

And you could make it even sadder by turning the boy into a puppy!

Huh?

A puppy! My secret to sadness has always been to take something sad, and then imagine it's happening to a poor little puppy dog with a broken leg.

It TOTALLY works! I just thought that losing a job would be sad, but a poor little injured puppy losing its job? That's heart-breaking!

LATER: T-REX TURNS UP THE CHARM!

Dromiceiomimus! I've come up with a new saddest thing ever!

What's that? T-Rex?

A universe where we never became friends.

Awww!

754

later after that: t-rex, using a pseudonym, publishes a whole series of picture books in which puppies break their legs and later get fired

t-rex is making fun of utahraptor and dromiceiomimus, but they're not around. he still gets the zinger in anyway. that's JUST HOW HE ROLLS

an alternate ending had t-rex opening an entire gender-themed restaurant. the restaurant sold things like patriarchy pie, and you might ask 'was there anything especially patriarchal about it?' the answer is, well, no, not especially.

I have started a radio show! It is an advice show. People can call me and I will give them advice on all of their problems, from being locked out of their house to being EMOTIONALLY locked out of their house in a RELATION-SHIP.

I call it, "I Know! I'll Ask T-Rex About My Stupid Problems!"

Do you think people will call into a show with that title, T-Rex? They'd be, you know, tacitly admitting that their problems are stupid.

This is a good thing! Stupid problems, like "I bought too much mayonnaise", are easy to solve. (The solution is to give away, return, or consume the extra mayonnaise.)

But what if people call in with real problems?

Easy: my mom answers them!

We're going to team up. I'll answer the silly questions, and there'll be a feature called "Ask T-Rex's Mom", where she'll answer all the hard questions. Moms are really good at things like that.

That's a really charming answer!

LATER, RECORDING "ASK T-REX'S MOM":
Dear Stranded On The Moon, that's an interesting problem you have there. It's almost as interesting as how a full grown T-Rex could forget Mother's Day.

Aw MOM!

even later: nobody likes mayonnaise, but everyone loves t-rex's mom!

757

T-REX PERHAPS WE CAN DISCUSS THE RELIGION THING LATER BUT FOR NOW WE MUST MAINTAIN OUR EYES ON
ULTIMATE GLORY OF THE SPEED RUN PRIZE

MORAL: if you are in trouble with someone, you could probably do worse than prepare them dinner?

meanwhile, in the present, t-rex struggles with the responsibilities inherent with the position of 'el presidente', including a 'tips and tricks' feature for the newsletter, managing the fundraising activities, and being visible in the community.

whenever i cook pasta, i sing 'la donna e mobile' (it's the opera song you're probably thinking of) while replacing all the lyrics with variations of 'if you like tasty things, you will like tasty things.' it's good times! for me!

although, upon closer inspection, 'What Do You Do When You Want To Give A Loved One A Present That Is Alive' would also make a pretty sweet title. can you imagine?

utahraptor gots SERIOUS problems when it comes to not screwing up those two phrases

incorporate cannibalism ONLY WHEN FEASIBLE, everybody

if you think t-rex's reaction to the pet duck is a little extreme, that's because you don't yet know that it's wearing an adorable duck-sized sailor uniform, complete with jaunty blue chapeau

i have this argument with my friends where i tell them i believe 'totally make out' means having sex, and they're all, no ryan, it just means making out to the EXTREME, and i say what's more EXTREME than having sex, and anyway, cool story huh

I have a new philosophy which is terrible AND compelling - arguably, the best kind of philosophy! Okay, so! Some dudes are stronger and/or smarter than other dudes, right?

Right! There are some tough and smart dudes!

BUT, none of them are so tough or so smart as to not be afraid of death (here we are ignoring sage Buddhist dudes who are probably not actually afraid of death). So! In a state of nature, everyone wants to avoid being killed, and so will defend themselves when faced with death. But since we need resources like food and water to live, and they're not infinite, we are constantly warring with one another for access to them.

Everyone is fighting everyone in an ENDLESS BATTLE FOR SURVIVAL!

And the only way out?

That's for us to realize that war sucks (it makes us die too), and so to give up a little of our freedom in exchange for an ABSOLUTE AUTHORITY who will ensure internal peace and common defence. Tada!

Wow, you've entirely ripped off Hobbes' Leviathan, in which he says EXACTLY THIS.

Not exactly this! He also says that life in the state of nature was "solitary, poor, nasty, brutish, and short", a compelling phrase unmatched by my poor offering of "sage Buddhist dudes". But I have a better phrase!

Is it once again time... FOR "SPOOKY PUBES"??

CHECK YOUR WATCHES, LADIES AND GENTLEMEN!!

Being tall in a world designed for average people can be sucky sometimes!

On account of the occasional back pain, that is!

Whoah, you get back pain? Mr. "I'm So Tough I Barely Miss Having Feelings?"

Sometimes! Only when I do the dishes. It's just because the counters at my house are designed for "norms", so I have to bend over to wash things in the sink!

("Norms" is what I call normal people, AND sets of guys named "Norm".)

Hey, can we segue this into talking about disabilities?

Sure, I guess!

ALTHOUGH, I'd rather if we didn't. There's a lot of issues and politics around disabilities (can deafness be something to be proud of? What do you make of strangers who volunteer to push you in your wheelchair?) and I'd rather not get involved in the debate via my being "super tall".

Okay nevermind!

LATER, T-REX GETS INVOLVED IN THE DEBATE ANYWAY:
Be it resolved that deaf couples should not be encouraged to adopt children who can hear.

HEY AN AUDIENCE MEMBER HAS SOME OPINIONS HE'D LIKE TO SHARE

ME

I'M THE AUDIENCE MEMBER

an alternate ending had t-rex calling his tallness a 'body feature' and then listing all the other features his body had, but then it ended up being pretty gross. body features more like BAWDY features

771

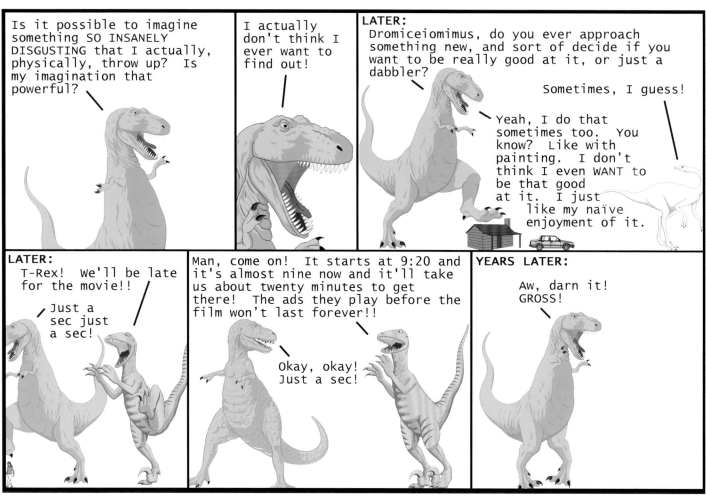

SCIENCE CORNER: if t-rex is telling the truth in panel three, then his kisses must consist mainly of water, proteins, carbohydrates, lipids, phospholipids, and electrolytes

I don't want anything bad to happen to my friends! I don't want anything bad to happen to people who aren't my friends either, but I don't want anything bad to happen to my friends IN PARTICULAR.

T-REX, UTAHRAPTOR AND DROMICEIOMIMUS STAR IN: COMICS!

The odds are that SOMEONE I know will be a victim of theft or crime or an accident or even violence, and that sucks, because there's basically nothing I can do to stop it!

You COULD stop it if you had absolute dominion over time and space, T-Rex.

You know I don't!!

You can't really live your life in fear of bad things happening, my friend!

Oh, it's not fear.

It's just - a preemptive sadness, I guess? Melancholy. By "melancholy" I mean "a thoughtful sadness", as opposed to the archaic definition ("a black bile once believed to be excreted by the kidneys").

I got that from context, yeah.

EPILOGUE:
I stomped on people while talking about how sad it is when bad things happen!

This is an example of "dramatic irony".

No it's not!

Utahraptor, you crazy dude! What are you doing in my epilogue?

this isn't breaking the fourth wall, because i currently have planned 'what are you doing in my epilogue' to be my last words, so people can say it in real life or whatever

775

I've come up with the best idea ever! Oh my goodness. LAUNDRY BAGS WITH GIANT GREEN DOLLAR SIGNS ON THEM. Hah hah! Am I robbing a bank in a cartoon or am I doing my laundry?

IT IS DIFFICULT TO TELL!

Are you planning to sell these bags to people who want to turn every laundry day into a chance for arrest, AND ALSO to those nostalgic for the charming visual shorthands of early cartoons?

I am indeed! Or at least, I was indeed, until I realized that you could just make your own with just a little fabric paint and a working knowledge of what dollar signs look like.

I actually think this has been done before T-Rex!

Aw man, really?

I did kinda suspect it might've been done before, since it seemed like a really funny idea, but I've never seen any such laundry bags! I'll just claim to have INDEPENDENTLY invented them.

Like how Alexander Graham Bell and that other dude both independently invented the telephone!

Yes! I will be that other dude! I will forever be immortalized as a "second place finisher" in history.

Wait, no, that sucks!

AMAZINGLY, 'wait, no, that sucks!' is exactly what elisha gray said when he found out that a.g. bell beat him to the telephone patent office by two hours.

MMM I DISMISS YOUR CONCERNS AS GRAPE JUICE FROM CONCENTRATE IS CLEARLY A DELICIOUS
BREAKFASTTIME TREAT

Wouldn't it be totally neat if life was more like a text-based adventure game?

"You look around and see that the answer is yes!"

It'd be great because people would have solid goals - nobody would be left wondering what to do with their lives!

But everyone would demand you do favours for them in exchange for inventory items!

Yeah! Plus, we'd have omniscient second-person narration!

Have you been talking to the Devil, T-Rex?

Nopers!

Huh! This really sounds like something he'd come up with. Anyway, I'm pretty sure this would be sucky, because we'd all be in bed thinking "get up" and then thinking "I don't see 'up' here", and then thinking "get out of bed", "stand up", and so on, until we hit on the right syntax to get ourselves moving. No thanks!

LATER, T-REX COMES ACROSS A GIANT CRUISE SHIP!

"take boat"

who among us has not seen a giant floating-city cruise ship and not wanted to, you know, just TAKE it?

I feel like I don't really have a solid opinion on the really big international issues. There's so much to them - so much nuance! How can I have a defensible opinion on something I don't fully understand?

However! I do have MANY unsolicited opinions on smaller, local issues!

Those issues I can understand completely, and there I DON'T feel like someone who just happens to know their stuff better could best me in an argument.

What kind of issues are you talking about?

Oh, you know - issues like "should mothers with baby carriages be allowed to be extreme."

EARLIER:
Man, did you see how extreme that mother was?

With the baby carriage? Yeah!

She was totally extreme.

I never saw a mother so extreme. Have you?

You know I would'a mentioned it to you if I had!

GUYS THAT MOTHER WAS SO EXTREME

God! Are there yet any laws against mothers being extreme, do you know?

NOT YET NOT TO THE BEST OF MY AWESOME KNOWLEDGE NO

780   t-rex is not sure where he stands on the conflict in the middle east, but he is FOR mothers with baby carriages being extreme.
you might wish to adopt these politics as your own.

if you were to ask dreamland t-rex what he'd like, he'd tell you, right away, he'd like to have just one discussion that didn't take a turn for the friggin' sexy

782

there is an embedded midi file of the ghostbusters theme song on an endless loop. ARGUABLY, such a feature should be included on every website.

(t-rex calls his mind the vault)

How come it's not cool to have stories with morals at the end anymore? Are we too ironic and COOL to appreciate a story that, you know, just straight-out tells you what to believe?

Seriously! How comes?

I liked it when you read a story and you knew that at the end, the moral would be spelled out for you in the last sentence, so you'd be sure you didn't miss anything. Does slow and steady win the race? Can this be clarified in the conclusion somehow?

You're saying you wish more literature was like fairy tales?

I guess so!

Well, instead of complaining about stories you don't like, why not write some that you do?

YES! And we'll have a "story-off" where we write stories and compete with each other!

Okay. I guess that's what I'm going to spend my life doing today.

AT THE "STORY OFF":
Once upon a time there was a bashful cat named "Neutron". He had so many fingers.

ADD A LOVE INTEREST!

It's my turn right now, T-Rex!

MY STORY HAS TWO LOVE INTERESTS

ROCCO AND CHOCO, THE TWINS! WHO! PUNCH!

this comic also works when you replace 'hunger' with other emotions, like 'sexy'. has constant sexy robbed you of all indentity? then this is the comic for you, my friend!

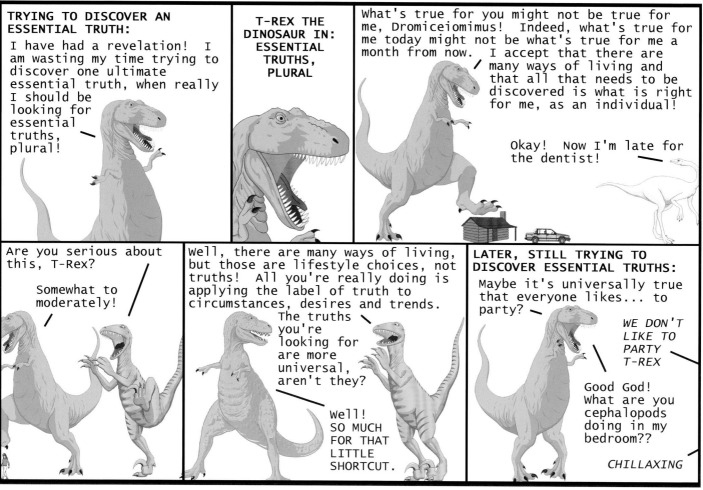

i took the final words of this comic from the final words of the one guy who ever witnessed a dude jump over a pit of bad dudes on a motorcycle, and then while he was over the pit, he hopped off the motorcycle and punched out all the bad dudes, and then he hopped back on the motorcycle, WHILE IT WAS STILL IN THE AIR!

t-rex and i share the same wide smile when we talk about weaponized kissing

The worst part of owning a cape is having to find excuses to wear it.

T-REX HAS A CAPE

LET'S SEE WHAT HAPPENS

Luckily, I am just the dude to manufacture such excuses! I have the perfect plan. Since it sucks to be the only dude in the room wearing a cape, I will simply start telling people that EXISTING holidays are now cape-wearing holidays. Like... Thanksgiving!

Thanksgiving?

Yes! It is now a day to give thanks AND wear stylish outmoded fashions.

NOW IT'S THANKSGIVING!

You forgot to wear your stupid cape, T-Rex!

Aw damn!!

But YOU forgot to wear it too, Utahraptor.

Yeah, but I was never going to.

Well! I certainly hope you'll change your mind for VAMPIRE DAY next week. I'm DEFINITELY not for-getting my cape for that!

NOW IT'S VAMPIRE DAY!

Aw damn!!

vampire day is a holiday t-rex invented where you all dress up as vampires and get bitey. it did not survive the cretaceous-tertiary extinction event?

791

Pantheism is the belief that everything, the entire universe, is literally God!

WHAT

Like I said! The universe and God are the exact same thing!

We all get to be divine, Dromiceiomimus! Better, everything I do is an act of God! Right now, THIS aspect of God wants to stomp on this other, more housey aspect of God.

I'm not sure that's how pantheism works! Isn't it more like, we're all cells in the "body" of a divine universe?

I see it more like, every tasty thing in the universe is God, and I'm getting HUNGRY.

T-Rex, you're just redefining "God" to mean "existence"!

Perhaps!

But PERHAPS by making everything special, by spreading that divinity around a bit so that everyone gets a piece, we'll all see our world as the extraordinary place it is.

Right. Or more likely, you just want to say "I'M GOD AND GOD WANTS GODLY SANDWICHES".

GOD DOES WANT GODLY SANDWICHES T-REX

Dude! It's not like you can't just make your own!

I LIKE IT WHEN YOU CUT OFF THE CRUSTS

dude makes some noticeably good sandwiches

TIPS FOR MEN

Attention men! Are you a man? Here are some tips!

Tip 1: Grooming is important!

This means that you have to shower and if you always wake up with food on your face then you have to understand that you have a problem. We all have problems, but yours is that you go to sleep beside bowls of wet salad and then in your sleep, you tip over the bowl. You need to work on that. I don't know what to tell you.

Tip 2: prostate exams: apparently important?

Apparently prostate exams are pretty important!

Tip 3: In some situations, like truck stops, manliness is measured by virility, so you may wish to boast of sexual conquests. But in other situations (job interviews), it's measured by problem solving skills and your ability to work in groups!

True men can easily distinguish between such situations.

TIPS FOR WOMEN

Attention women! Sometimes men fall asleep next to bowls of wet salad. I don't know what to tell you.

here is a persuasive writing tip from utahraptor: if you are writing an essay and want to say 'everything' without having to defend it, write 'most everything'. it means 'a lot of things' but sounds like 'everything' to the casual reader! with this in your 'bag of writerly tricks', you will have certain success in EVERYTHING YOU EVER DO.

Okay, so perhaps there ARE those who find old jokes in old books to be hilarious, and we just happen to have different senses of humour! IT MAY HAVE BEEN A MISTAKE TO GENERALIZE ACROSS EVERY LIVING THING THAT CAN LAUGH, AND ALSO READ.

This I do concede!

But, I still think that it's true that, given a random joke from the present and one from the past, the average person will be more likely to laugh at the present joke, just because they have more context. I'm convinced present-day jokes about airplane food will fade in cultural relevance and become less funny as airplanes are replaced by HoverPants!

Hey, nice move, T-Rex!

Ah, you refer to my classy search for a middle ground!

No, I meant the whole "shift the argument to the future" thing, so that nobody can disagree with you! It was smooth.

Hee, it's true! It's the same argument, but since the future doesn't exist yet, nobody can really argue with me one way or the other!

MEANWHILE, IN THE FUTURE:

The hell? What was I saying about us not existing?

I dunno man!

I would have words with past T-Rex! That dude has a lot of STALE FRIGGIN' OPINIONS.

future t-rex is always one-step ahead! BA DUM DUM CHING

797

this is a crazy comic about how t-rex likes the kanye west song from a while ago. have you heard the song? it's pretty catchy, and it's about a woman who digs for gold, totally metaphorically!

it is the best result that t-rex can muster under very difficult physiological circumstances okay

THINGS THAT CAN COST YOU A LIFETIME OF FRIENDSHIP: rampant murderism, incurable stealie-o-holicism, terminal punchiness

dude loves his breakfast, you don't even know

> use SPACESHIPS on TERRESTRIAL PROBLEMS to shift them to a future where we might be able to properly solve them
> i don't see SPACESHIPS here.

Hey! Hey Utahraptor! Do - do you think that some guys go to liquor stores to pick up chicks because they know everyone there is over 18?

Or at least -

- willing to pretend?

Hah! Aw! That's terrible, T-Rex!

Dromiceiomimus, what are YOU doing here? I thought it was Just The Guys!

It seems that, once again, I have become privy to guy talk due to conversational negligence!!

Disaster!

EARLIER:
So personally, Dromiceiomimus, I feel that -

Hey, where is she?

Whoah, Utahraptor! I thought that DROMICEIOMIMUS was behind me!

Nope! Just me, your male friend Utahraptor! Were you about to have a conversation about feelings?

NO. NO I WASN'T.

"SOME PEOPLE TREAT THEIR GENDERED FRIENDS DIFFERENTLY"

Incidentally, I don't have any friends who aren't gendered!

OKAY

when t-rex gets angry he likes to shout the name of the person or thing that made him so upset into his communicator!
unfortunately captain kirk and khan have already taken care of THAT little number

I am writing the best story ever! In it, I simply APPROPRIATE a popular novel, and then place its author in a generalized version of its premise! THEN, the author has eerily familiar, but thoroughly modernized, adventures.

So, it's like, H.G. Wells actually has a time machine that he uses for wacky escapades!

And then he goes back in time to meet Edgar Allan Poe, who actually IS haunted by the supernatural and has a creepy raven in his study, next to the silken sad uncertain rustling of his purple curtains. After picking up Mary Shelley, they ALL go forward in time and meet Patricia Highsmith, who is surrounded by morally compromised antihero neighbours! Then they all go on a train ride and have an adventure.

Then what happens?

THEN, my friend, the story writes itself!

And at the end, all the characters high five each other and go home to their own times, promising to write their own versions of what happened. Then, they all write their most famous works!

Huh!

MUCH LATER:

Edgar Allan Poe! What are YOU doing here?

I'm just chillin' on your couch, T-Rex!

Awesome! I like how you rhyme.

t-rex was going to suggest that they play video games together, but then poe was like, 't-rex! i am from the past!'

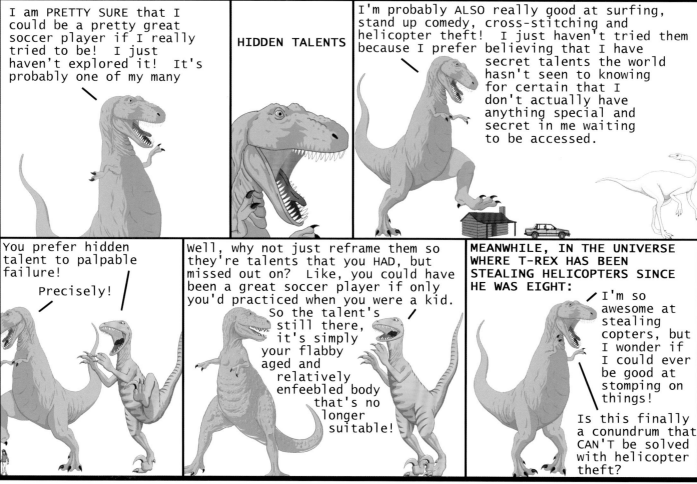

I am PRETTY SURE that I could be a pretty great soccer player if I really tried to be! I just haven't explored it! It's probably one of my many

HIDDEN TALENTS

I'm probably ALSO really good at surfing, stand up comedy, cross-stitching and helicopter theft! I just haven't tried them because I prefer believing that I have secret talents the world hasn't seen to knowing for certain that I don't actually have anything special and secret in me waiting to be accessed.

You prefer hidden talent to palpable failure!

Precisely!

Well, why not just reframe them so they're talents that you HAD, but missed out on? Like, you could have been a great soccer player if only you'd practiced when you were a kid. So the talent's still there, it's simply your flabby aged and relatively enfeebled body that's no longer suitable!

MEANWHILE, IN THE UNIVERSE WHERE T-REX HAS BEEN STEALING HELICOPTERS SINCE HE WAS EIGHT:

I'm so awesome at stealing copters, but I wonder if I could ever be good at stomping on things!

Is this finally a conundrum that CAN'T be solved with helicopter theft?

every single problem this t-rex, up til now, has been solved through stealing a helicopter. so what i'm saying is IT'S BEEN A GOOD RUN

seriously he's the worst ghost ever. if you knew him you'd know!

hey t-rex sure dodged a bullet there in panel three, RIGHT FELLAS?

this one goes out to all the brothers and mothers who have come up with ideas that can only make the world a worse place. hey, here's to not implementing them!

THINGS WOMEN LOVE:
I know all sorts of things women love! For example: Women LOVE IT when you dismiss them in arguments by saying "Whoah! This kitten's got claws!"

ACTUALLY NOBODY LOVES IT WHEN YOU SAY THAT T-REX

No way dude!

It's hilarious! It's IRONIC, because I've never actually called a woman a "kitten", on account of how I'm not a facial hair dude from the seventies? And it also says "I understand you're upset, but not REALLY upset, because I'm willing to make a joke that's sort of at your expense, but also really at my own expense too, because now I look like a sexist facial hair dude! Let's share a laugh!"

There are layers upon layers!

So you're using sexism ironically now!

Yep! But it's not SINCERE sexism. I wouldn't say, "Whoah! This cute, somehow inferior gender's got claws!"

And you'd laugh if a woman said something similar, but at the expense of men, to you.

PROBABLY. It's never happened!

UTAHRAPTOR ASKS DROMICEIOMIMUS TO HELP HIM OUT BUT FAILS TO BRIEF HER PROPERLY:

Whoah! This dog's got breasts!

I wanna see!

they must be noticeable in some way is t-rex's instant, sincerely-felt conclusion

you know how sometimes you have an idea for a pun and you just run with it against everyone else's good advice?
THIS IS ONE SUCH TIME MY PRETTIES

now folks can't get mad at me for tacitly endorsing funny wikipedia vandalism because fictional jimbo wales HIMSELF is all for it. good ol' fictional jimbo wales! he is the most accomodating instance of jimbo wales that i know of.

how come 'kant's categorical imperative' isn't spelt with a 'k' on 'kategorical'? think we all know who dropped the ball here: IMMANUEL KANT. more like immanuel kant recognize spelling opportunities in a non-native tongue when he sees them, amiright?

i knew this guy where when he got seriously disappointed he started to bruise. prognosis: that's gross.

Hey God, would the world be an even awesomer place if everyone named "Benjamin" instead when by the name "Ben Jammin'"

DEFINITELY YES

See, THAT'S what I keep telling everyone!

I'm so glad I was right on this one.

Do you know any Benjamins, T-Rex?

Nope! I knew one when I was a kid, but he moved away way before I ever found out about jammin'. That was in - what, grade 5?

THE END

SPECIAL "HEY, WHATEVER HAPPENED TO BEN" SECTION:

Hey, whatever happened to Ben?

WELL, last I heard he was starting high school a few towns over, so I presume he went through the development process that is high school and emerged a changed, taller man than the person I remember from our halcyon pre-pubescent days.

Sounds plausible!

Another case closed!

And by that I mean, "That was my first experience with losing a friend!"

special 'hey, whatever happened to high school' section: time magazine canadian edition says that NOW, kids use technologies like THE INTERNET and INSTANT MESSENGER PROGRAMS to communicate to each other outside of the watchful eyes of teachers, and expresses concern about 'cyber bullying'. thanks, time magazine canadian edition.

What should I do if I see someone littering? Every time I do something different and every time it feels like the wrong thing to do.

LITTERING COMICS

all over the internet

and this book as well

I've tried doing nothing, but that left me feeling like a frustrated milquetoast pushover! I keep wanting to pull the "excuse me, you dropped this" line, but it is sort of an aggressive thing to do, especially if the way I say it makes it clear I think it was, indeed, NO ACCIDENT. I could see that leading to a confrontation, and I don't want to be that guy who throws punches over empty cans of Coke!

You could throw down over disgusting used Kleenexes!

But it's an overreaction, isn't it?

I don't know - littering's this perfectly situated thing where it's not THAT big a deal taken individ-ually, but a really antisocial thing when taken on a larger scale.

And yet, not really, when you compare it to, say, murderin' dudes.

Exactly! I don't know how I should react when confronted with a small instance of a small crime, but which still bothers me. All I can think of is to sneak poo bugs into the dude's food?

Poo bugs aren't an all-purpose revenge tool, T-Rex.

You take that back!!

820

this goes out to the girl i saw on youtube who said she wanted to be a webcartoonist and used the word 'dudes'.
ATTENTION BOOK READERS: I AM LIVING THE DREAM

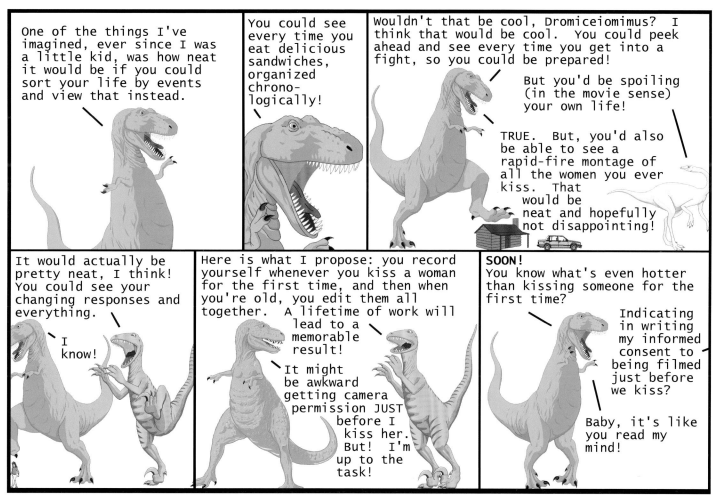

THE PERFECT WOMAN????

LOGICAL FALLACY COMICS
today's fallacy:
PLURIUM INTERROGATIONUM

"the loaded question"

A "loaded question" is when you ask a question that presupposes something unproven!

For instance, Dromiceiomimus, I could ask, "Hey, Dromiceiomimus! Are you still punching children?"

What? No!!

Aha - so when did you stop? See what I did there? The question presupposes that you've been punching on children in the past, and goes on to suggest that maybe you're still doing so. It is LOADED like rich Uncle Pennybags. From Monopoly?

Your question is really two questions combined into one!

Yep!

It breaks down to "Have you ever punched children, and, if so, are you still doing so?" But since these are merged, and since this merged form still demands a yes or no answer, "no" becomes misleading. The solution is not to answer "yes" or "no", but to reject the question!

Really!

T-Rex, are YOU still punchin' children? Are you still punching them just to steal their ice cream cones?

I reject your question, Utahraptor! It's loaded!

Why are you SO AFRAID of the truth coming out, T-Rex?

Okay you must never enter politics ever.

kids are like, 'ow! fine, here, take the damn ice cream'

hey! t-rex sincerely believes that any song about bitches can be changed to a song about your male acquaintances by replacing 'bitches' with 'fellows'. where my fellows at? fellows ain't shit like hoes and tricks!

you may want to read innuendo into panel three. i can't stop you! shit! it's a free internet!
this book probably cost you money though!

826

the devil is asking for a friend of his. they were playing video games and all of a sudden the guy asked 'do you ever feel bad about your body?' and the sudden implied intimacy was startling, coming from an acquaintance, maybe a near friend, who had previously only asked him to stop hogging all the powerups. the devil didn't know what to say so he laughed it off, and they finished the game and both acted as if everything was fine, but the question, and the way it made him feel, has lingered with him ever since.

I think that I have a few friends, "Super Friends", if you will, that I'll keep in touch with no matter what happens, and they with me. It comforts me to think this!

T-REX AND HIS SUPER FRIENDS

Dromiceiomimus, you are one such super friend! I can see us getting together years from now, after we all drift apart, and still being able to pick up from where we left off. We'd email once or twice a year and that would be all it would take to maintain our super friendship.

Aww! I agree!

You're one of MY super friends, T-Rex!

And you're one of mine, of course!

Sweet! We're all friends, and super friends at that, which I guess really just goes to show you that you don't need conflict to drive a narrative.

What narra-

THE NARRATIVE OF LIFE.

MEANWHILE, IN THE UNIVERSE WHERE T-REX WATCHES THIS OTHER T-REX'S LIFE ON TV:

where are the knockers

alternate ending: utahraptor says 'So - you want to be able to love ads, but also don't want marketers to benefit from this love?' and t-rex replies, 'Yes! Is there no way to satiate my perfectly compatible desires?' and then there's no real solution THE END

SUDDENLY: REMORSE!

Aw, I feel kinda bad about taking advantage of Captain Suggestible. What do you do with someone who is that damn suggestible?

Dude has his own problems!

It reminds me of this friend I had in high school who could never ever detect sarcasm, no matter what. It's such a small thing, but it would come up all the time when I'd be like, "oh, no, please, no more ketchup!" and then I wouldn't get any more ketchup when ACTUALLY I wanted some more ketchup.

That came up all the time?

We were CRAZY DUDES in high school!!

So you see Captain Suggestible as a tragic figure?

Maybe! Mostly I see elements of myself.

He's just got this big interpersonal thing where he's not quite sure what's appropriate, and because of that he transgresses unwritten societal boundaries all the time. I think we've all done that a little, and it's embarrassing!

Ah, you refer to last Saturday night, when you went nude swimming "by accident".

LAST SATURDAY NIGHT:

EVERYONE! OBSERVE MY BEACH NUDITY!

THIS IS NO ACCIDENT

ryan can we have one comic about serious issues without full frontal PLEASE

829

okay okay god should really be saying 'the exact opposite of how SOME religions work', but that makes the punchline have a terminal case of the NOT FUNNIES

number six in the meandering 'for teens' series, coming after 'Proper Manners', 'Third Dates', 'Human Sexuality', 'Sawing' and 'Overseas Correspondence by Post'

831

There is a lawyer dude who has plastered the city's telephone poles and bus shelters with ads proclaiming "QUICK DIVORCE! $300". And there's always about 2 or 3 of the little phone numbers from the bottom taken!

Ouch for modern marriages!

I took one, but that was simply because I saw the HILARIOUS PRANK POSSIBILITIES of leaving one in a married friend's wallet. But then I had an EVEN BETTER idea! Next to each of his divorce fliers, I put up my own that say "QUICK MARITAL BLISS! $295.95". Hah hah! It is PUBLIC SPACE ART and it also makes bus shelters less depressingly pro-quick-divorce!

Nice!

So what happens when people start to call you, T-Rex?

What?

What happens when people start to call you? They'll probably be expecting some quick marital bliss for their $295.95!

I, um - I hadn't thought of that. I was too impressed with having an actual good idea for an art project to think about "consequences"!

LUCKILY, T-REX DISCOVERS A SURE-FIRE WAY TO TURN $295.95 INTO QUICK MARITAL BLISS:

Thanks, T-Rex!! You've saved our sucky marriage once again!

Hah hah!

How perfectly PROFITABLE!

what's this? two tickets to amnesia land?

Time for me to learn some new languages! AS THE OLD SAYING GOES, he who can speak many languages is suspected by his peers to be an ultra super genius times two.

Perhaps I will learn... SIGN LANGUAGE?

Oh, you should, T-Rex! Then we could talk to each other!

You know sign language?

Yep! Well - I know Signed English, which is just English translated into hand signs. It's different from ASL, which is a true natural signed language with its own grammar!

Neat!

Then it's settled! I will learn sign language!

And I will learn Zulu!

I've always wanted to learn a language nobody around me speaks, and I like the way Zulu sounds.

Dude, maybe we're TRENDSETTERS! Maybe in 3 months languages less spoken will be the very CURRENCY of coolness, a shibboleth for entry into the rarefied world of ULTRA POPULARITY!

That only works if we're ultra popular, but we're just two dudes who have decided in the past 60 seconds to learn some new languages for no real reason!

My question: WHAT COULD BE COOLER THAN THAT??

a: having your own hat?

833

if i were a sleazy guy, i would use my, 'if i were you, i'd tell my friends about me' line ALL THE TIME. i'd have it printed on business cards! i'd hand them out to women i just met while stealing sips of their drinks.

I am a dude who came across a suitcase full of old love letters I got in high school. Sweet!

That's right, ladies! I'VE got a HISTORY!

I'd completely forgotten about these letters, and it was really cool to re-read them now with older, less hormonally-charged eyes! We were crazy kids struggling with feelings we didn't fully understand. It was charming! Also, and I, um, I don't pretend to understand this, but there's one letter from each girlfriend where, without exception, she's drawn the two of us, she and I, as Batman and the Joker.

Hah! How many girlfriends were there?

I refuse to say!!

But I assure you that for whatever reason, each of them saw it fit to render a copyright-infringing vision of a universe where we live the astonishing dreams of Finger and Kane.

That's really odd, isn't it? What do you suppose it means?

Man! I think that's pretty obvious!

Everyone I've ever kissed is AWESOME!

THE UNIVERSE WHERE EVERYTHING COMES BACK TO TOAST:
So yeah, as I was saying, the relativist fallacy is when you reject a claim by saying "Oh, that may be true for you, but it's not true for me."

HUH

But you have to be careful: the fallacy only applies to objective facts!

So if I say "the atomic mass of xenon is 131.3 AMU", a response of "Oh, maybe it is for YOU!" is a fallacy. But if I said "toast is the ultimate breakfast-time treat", you could very well respond with "maybe for YOU, not for ME" and it wouldn't be a fallacy, because as we know the debate over breakfast is as subjective as it is eternal.

Who are you explaining the relativist fallacy to?

Oh, just God!

He was asking me what the weight of xenon was and I was all "Duh, 131.3 AMU" and he was all "Duh, maybe for you, T-Rex" and I was all, "Aha! Time to pontificate!" Then I worked in an example about toast.

HEY! Let's go get some toast!

It all comes back to toast!

every conversation in this universe ends like that. you might think it gets tiring, but nope!

okay cannibals in my audience listen i'm sorry but i'm pretty sure you're not throwing in with the laws of god and man

in real life truth serum doesn't really exist! that and talking dinosaurs is all that separates my comic from the real world

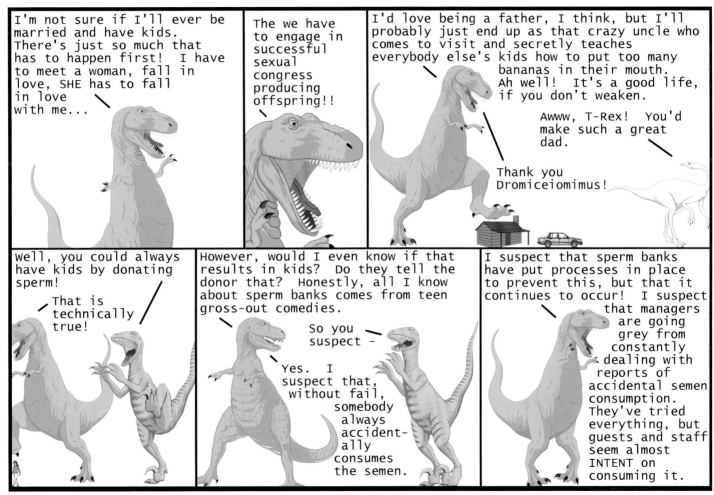

I'm not sure if I'll ever be married and have kids. There's just so much that has to happen first! I have to meet a woman, fall in love, SHE has to fall in love with me...

The we have to engage in successful sexual congress producing offspring!!

I'd love being a father, I think, but I'll probably just end up as that crazy uncle who comes to visit and secretly teaches everybody else's kids how to put too many bananas in their mouth. Ah well! It's a good life, if you don't weaken.

Awww, T-Rex! You'd make such a great dad.

Thank you Dromiceiomimus!

Well, you could always have kids by donating sperm!

That is technically true!

However, would I even know if that results in kids? Do they tell the donor that? Honestly, all I know about sperm banks comes from teen gross-out comedies.

So you suspect -

Yes. I suspect that, without fail, somebody always accident-ally consumes the semen.

I suspect that sperm banks have put processes in place to prevent this, but that it continues to occur! I suspect that managers are going grey from constantly dealing with reports of accidental semen consumption. They've tried everything, but guests and staff seem almost INTENT on consuming it.

they're beginning to wonder if they're the weird ones for just having a salad for lunch.

839

Hmm... what's the biggest mistake I've ever made, I wonder?

More broccoli, please!

Oh, whatever! That wasn't even a mistake. I've got to tally up a lifetime of failings and concentrate HARDER THAN EVER BEFORE! I will stomp on things to focus my mental energies, or "menergies".

What about the time you built the Riverboat Shabby, T-Rex?

Hmm...!

This riverboat has so many holes, T-Rex! It's so shabby!

Hah hah!

No way!

Now we're sinking because of how shabby this boat is!

Hah hah hah!

What?

man you go on the miaden cruise of something called 'the riverboat shabby', you are asking for sinky surprises

Here is a terrible idea for a date: you take the lady to a stinky old sewage processing plant and then tour the facilities! You could be all, "Sorry, potential lifemate!! I'm a dude who makes bad date decisions."

T-REX AND FRIENDS IN: "DATES"

I bet most sewage processing plants are actually cool and don't really smell like poops, T-Rex! It would probably end up being a pretty good AND informative date. How does waste reclamation work anyway?

Huh! I don't know, Dromiceiomimus!

It is essentially awesome, my friend!

Oh yeah?

Yeah! A combination of physical (letting the heavy bits settle), biological, and chemical means are often used. Sometimes they even create artificial swamps to attract animals that aid in the waste reclamation process!

Neat!

LATER, A DATE TO A WASTE RECLAMATION FACILITY!

You are so charming, T-Rex! And I LOVE learning about waste reclamation!

I feel the same way, T-Rex!

Wow, you are one appreciative date, and YOU are one surprisingly amorous tour guide!!

hey t-rex's last line is something we've all said before, right fellas?

Excuse me, sir!! This bill you gave me is counterfeit!

Aw snapadoodle!

"COUNTERFEIT BILLS COMICS"

So then I just gave her a new bill. It was a little embarrassing, but my REAL problem is what to do with this fiver, now that I know it's a fake!

Spending it would just shift the problem onto somebody else.

Exactly! And bringing it to a bank just means I'm out $5; they wouldn't exchange it for a real bill because then the counterfeiters could just go to the banks too.

I think you are an unfortunate victim without recourse of CURRENCY CRIME, my friend!

Aw poo.

The best you can do is report it to the police and be more vigilant in the future. Unless you're willing to further the crime by passing it off as legal tender, I'm afraid you're out the five dollars.

Man! You know where I got the fake money? Change from a friggin' fast food restaurant.

I blame the Colonel Sanders!

COLONEL SANDERS HAS BEEN ADDED TO YOUR REVENGE LIST

Well good!

842

counterfeit bill comics are distinct from counterfeit bill's comics, which are comics made by counterfeit bill, that loveable scamp with the tin can shoes

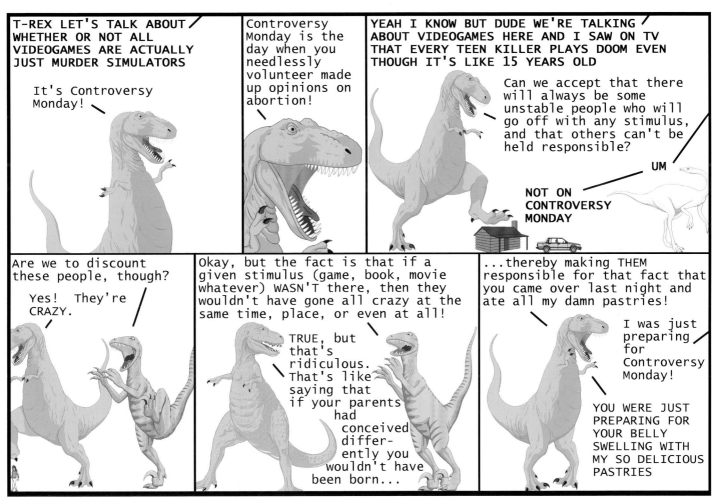

T-REX LET'S TALK ABOUT WHETHER OR NOT ALL VIDEOGAMES ARE ACTUALLY JUST MURDER SIMULATORS

It's Controversy Monday!

Controversy Monday is the day when you needlessly volunteer made up opinions on abortion!

YEAH I KNOW BUT DUDE WE'RE TALKING ABOUT VIDEOGAMES HERE AND I SAW ON TV THAT EVERY TEEN KILLER PLAYS DOOM EVEN THOUGH IT'S LIKE 15 YEARS OLD

Can we accept that there will always be some unstable people who will go off with any stimulus, and that others can't be held responsible?

UM

NOT ON CONTROVERSY MONDAY

Are we to discount these people, though?

Yes! They're CRAZY.

Okay, but the fact is that if a given stimulus (game, book, movie whatever) WASN'T there, then they wouldn't have gone all crazy at the same time, place, or even at all!

TRUE, but that's ridiculous. That's like saying that if your parents had conceived differently you wouldn't have been born...

...thereby making THEM responsible for that fact that you came over last night and ate all my damn pastries!

I was just preparing for Controversy Monday!

YOU WERE JUST PREPARING FOR YOUR BELLY SWELLING WITH MY SO DELICIOUS PASTRIES

did you know that monarchs, like all butterflies, are SCIENTIFICALLY INCAPABLE OF IMAGINATION?? this forever bars them from dreamland

Here are some professions whose female members I could never marry because I'd be such an uncontrollably bad husband to them!

First: dentists!

I respect what they do but I'm sorry lady oral hygiene professionals, I can't brush and floss three times a day plus after every snack, drink, or intense fantasy about food. I have tried and failed! Also I couldn't marry a professional housecleaner because she would soon suspect that I'm obsessed with trying to undermine all that she's striving for with my every discarded sock and unwashed dish!

I like how you imagine everyone is so attached to their job!

Oh yeah?

Yeah! It's like you can't imagine a universe where someone could be a dentist but not actually really be all that into teeth, or a cleaner who doesn't despise disorder. Jobs are all done because of joy and intense personal conviction!

That's because I choose the universe I want to live in.

I ALSO believe all conflicts are solvable through communication, peace is attainable, and that love is a gift that cannot be commodified!

What happens if these turn out not to be true?

Then I mourn the death of childhood and my final loss of innocence!!

Duh!

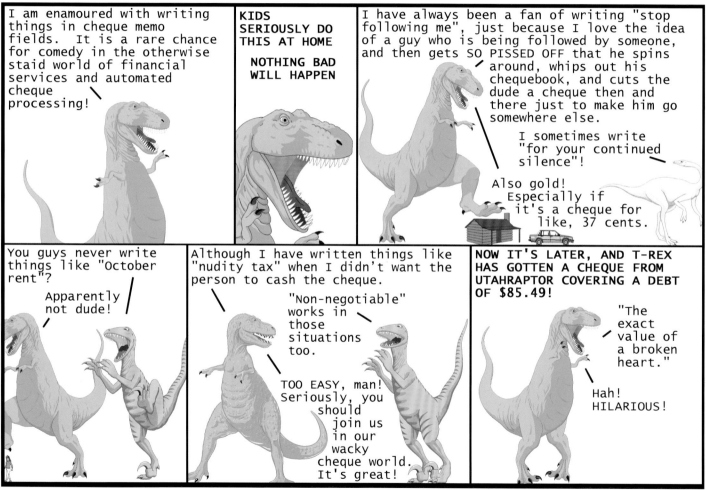

I am enamoured with writing things in cheque memo fields. It is a rare chance for comedy in the otherwise staid world of financial services and automated cheque processing!

KIDS SERIOUSLY DO THIS AT HOME

NOTHING BAD WILL HAPPEN

I have always been a fan of writing "stop following me", just because I love the idea of a guy who is being followed by someone, and then gets SO PISSED OFF that he spins around, whips out his chequebook, and cuts the dude a cheque then and there just to make him go somewhere else.

I sometimes write "for your continued silence"!

Also gold! Especially if it's a cheque for like, 37 cents.

You guys never write things like "October rent"?

Apparently not dude!

Although I have written things like "nudity tax" when I didn't want the person to cash the cheque.

"Non-negotiable" works in those situations too.

TOO EASY, man! Seriously, you should join us in our wacky cheque world. It's great!

NOW IT'S LATER, AND T-REX HAS GOTTEN A CHEQUE FROM UTAHRAPTOR COVERING A DEBT OF $85.49!

"The exact value of a broken heart."

Hah! HILARIOUS!

americans: 'cheque' is how the rest of the english-speaking world spells the word 'check'. i know!
you guys sure don't like the letter 'u'!

I have another genius plan for immortality!

BUT THOSE PLANS NEVER WORK T-REX

This time for sure!

I will be remembered in the CULTURAL ZEITGEIST. And this time I won't even have to do anything memorable! I will simply become famous by virtue of my being famous. I will construct a synthetic celebrity and I will reap the benefits!

But won't you be remembered as someone that nobody actually liked?

I am hoping to be remembered as "the dude with the confusing allure".

So how do you become famous in the first place, then?

Huh?

Oh, I must have explained it poorly. I'll just act like I'm famous, you know, get people to react to me like I'm famous, and then kapow! We have CRITICAL MASS for actual fame.

And I'm the guy who's going to be asked to act like you're famous?

You guess correctly!!

LATER:
Wow, is that T-Rex. He's the dude with the confusing allure, and I want to find out more?

Aw, come on!! You're not even punctuating it properly!

alternate last line: t-rex just says 'damn, dude! diggity daaaaaaamn!!' THE END

847

The Uncanny Valley is the name given to the idea that as we build robots that look more and more like real people, the more we approach a point where we all say "oh God oh God what is wrong with that robot where did it all go wrong OH GOD".

This also applies to animation!

The idea is that crudely-realized characters don't look like real people, but we can see some qualities of real people in them, so they're cute! But as you add more and more realism without quite reaching perfection, you reach a point where suddenly instead of cartoons that look real, they're real people who look TERRIBLY WRONG. Cuteness is replaced with the same reaction we'd have to a putrid, retching, animated corpse: revulsion, and the question "why??".

But if you can make the characters look even better, you get past that!

True!

Hence the "valley" - you accept the creature more and more, then are suddenly repulsed, then you accept it the most.

Perhaps... a powerful metaphor for LOVE?

Hah! I don't think I love the way you do!

LATER, AT HALLOWE'EN!
There! My costume looks like a failed corpse that still makes a blasphemous claim to life. Thanks, Uncanny Valley!

No problem, T-Rex!

It's so upsetting that you got personified, Uncanny Valley.

848

t-rex isn't trying to be rude, it's just - it's so upsetting that the uncanny valley got personified.

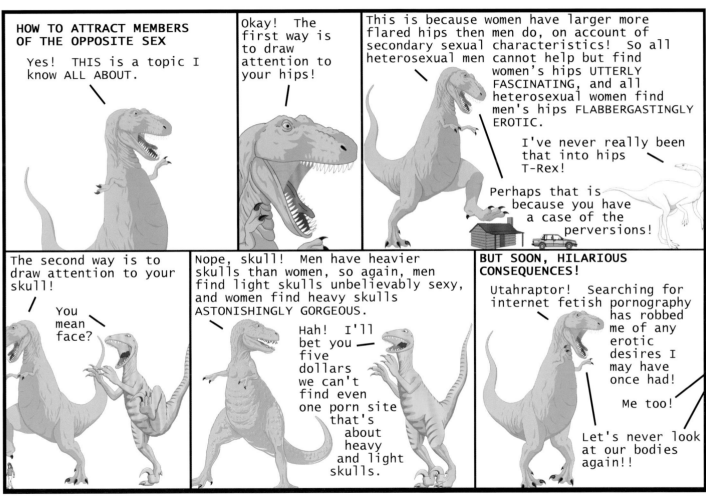

have you ever searched for porn sites with your best friend just to settle a bet? if you have then okay! you don't need to brag about it. god. i was just asking.

BACKSTORY: there's a new game called 'ultimate real-life road trip simulator' and the devil wants to know if it's worth downloading the shareware version because his dsl is out so he's on dialup and the file is about 50 megs and on 2400 baud that's like two whole days of tying up the phone line so is it worth it is his question

MMM T-REX I'VE NOT YET EXPERIENCED A NON-VIRTUAL ROAD TRIP AND WAS WONDERING IF CAN YOU TELL ME WHAT THEY ARE LIKE

In one sentence starting with "Dude"?

FINE

Dude, road trips rule!

What's special about them is that it's a time when you and your friends can sit together in a single place for literally hours and chat, but protracted silences don't need to be filled. You can just look out the windows or nap! If you were all in a blank room somewhere, it would be weird to just sit there and stare at the walls, but the ever-changing scenery in a car provides a distraction that is both welcomed and also easy to interrupt. There's nothing like it!

An idea: we should all go on a road trip!

Yes!! I agree!

I vote we trip to: Brazil!

That's pretty far. How about someplace closer?

THE ISLAND CONTINENT OF AUSTRALIA??

We'd need a car that works on water for that.

Okay! But Utahraptor, what's that across the street? A car that works on water??

aw come on you guys it's mine

Jacques Esqueleto!! I thought I made you up!

later, the devil is all alone and he says 'THAT WAS AS GOOD AN EXPLANATION AS I DESERVE'.

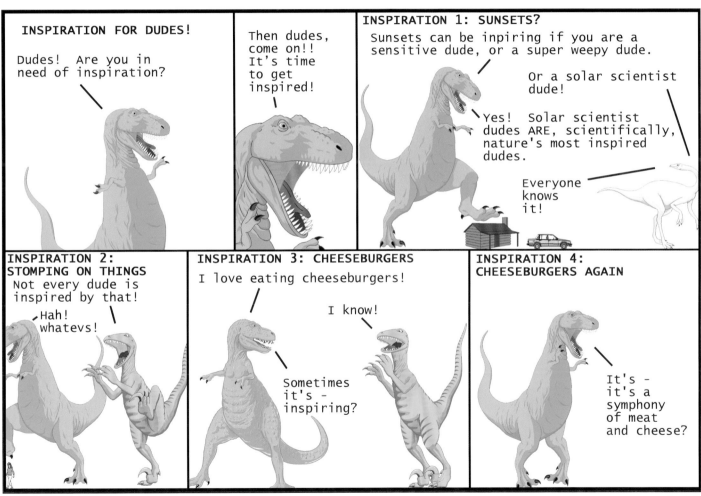

this comic is inspired by my friend chris and his remarkable, remorseless, and above all truly inspiring love of meat and cheese.

if you don't fantasize in pixelated IM conversations then um, what are you waiting for

HOW TO PASS THE TURING TEST

a helpful comic for machine intelligences that "just have trouble in test situations"

The Turing test is a test that all emergent intelligences face at one point or another!

In it, you have a REAL person engaged in a text conversation with both a person and a machine, and that person has to determine which responder is which. If the machine can appear more "alive" than the person, then they pass!

And then they're officially conscious?

Nope! The problem is that the test doesn't prove consciousness, just communication, and um, it can be faked.

Oh man - you're going to say "brute force"! You're going to use the brute force approach!

Hells yes!

Since conversations don't last forever, then there's a finite number of sentences that make sense and that are at least passibly grammatical, so you can just record every possible response to every possible word combination, and kapow! Responses like a real person.

Man! That's lame.

What's lame? We've just totally faked out the Turing test and all it required was near infinite storage space!

Brute force: the approach of kings and the king of approaches?

I disagree!

Tell me more about DISAGREE?

854   i thought i invented this cheat but philosopher Ned Block beat me to the punch here, and the machine he imagines to do this is called 'blockhead', which, i concede, is a pretty awesome name for a made-up universe-sized computer

Oh man, am I ever sick. Me! I never get sick but this time I've gotten sick.

My mighty body lies in shambles!

Oh, Dromiceiomimus, you've got to save me! Failing that, tell them my story. Regale future generations with stories of Mighty T-Rex, felled by nothing greater than the common cold. Irony will be my theme, stomping my leitmotif!!

You've got a runny nose?

Oh, and a headache too! This is how my story ends: not in a bang but a sniffle. For shame!

Can I tell people your story?

Dromiceiomimus is APPARENTLY UNWILLING, so yes!

Excellent! I'M going to shoehorn my own politics into your tale, reducing you to a mere representation of Heidegger and the story to transparent lecturing in which characters often break the fourth wall to tell my readers what they should believe!

Aw dude! You're imagining it right now!!

I represent Heidegger! Watch as I stomp on "the little guy" who's just trying to understand my seemingly purposely obscure philosophical writing!

Wow! Utahraptor is right in everything he says!

You said it, everyone!

if you don't know him, heidegger is a 20th century philosopher who is nototriously difficult to read. this is me:
'haha ouch heidegger sorry you're so hard to read dude :o'

Your search - "dudes forsooth" - did not match any documents.

Do you get to write your own epitaph? If you do, then mine will seriously be "Here lies T-Rex: the radical dude with the radical 'tude!" Or even "T-Rex: smart and trim; let's be like him"!

T-REX'S BUSY DAY

Aw, you're always on about epitaphs, T-Rex! How about something new, like - instead of a sentence people remember you by, an image? Say, 10 seconds of silent video!

That's neat! You could cheat and have 1920s title cards ("DUDES, FORSOOTH! I'M SO DEAD") but just silent images would also be cool. What would you have?

A kid in a tree, and then the tree becomes enormous, and the kid is happy about that.

Hmm! I guess I'd have a picture of me giving a thumbs up.

Lame!

You didn't let me finish! THEN, over me and my thumbs up, a newspaper spins towards the camera 1930s style, fills the frame, and the headline says "T-REX AWESOME, DEAD!"

Huh - not bad, actually! Do me.

Okay! Let me think...

Alright - YOURS would be a video of a soggy dog, and then the dog throws up a little, and then there's a subtitle that says "BAD DECISIONS".

Okay I'm putting in my will that you can't ever do a video epitaph for me.

That's tough, yet fair!

t-rex nobody spoke like that in the 1920s or ever, come on, let's be SERIOUS

DIFFERENT WAYS TO SAY GOODBYE:

Later!

THAT WAY'S OKAY

NEVER USE THIS WAY PLEASE:

Compadres! I bid you each... ADIEU!

THIS WAY IS ALSO PRETTY TERRIBLE:
It's not "goodbye", just - "farewell". This isn't the end, Dromiceiomimus, but merely the end of an era. One door closes as another opens, and we can't forever live in the past! A new, brighter tomorrow beckons.

I DON'T KNOW WHERE T-REX IS GOING WITH THIS. IT IS JUST ONE CLICHÉ AFTER ANOTHER. IF I COULD TALK TO T-REX I WOULD SAY,
HELLO T-REX, WHAT IS THE DEAL.

HERE'S A GOOD WAY:
Hasta la vista, tiny woman!

Stop it, T-Rex!

THAT WAS GOOD BECAUSE WE ALL SAW TERMINATOR 2. THAT WAS A PRETTY GOOD MOVIE

I liked it.

Oh my God, me too!!

ANYWAY IT IS NOT THAT HARD TO SAY GOODBYE.

THE ONLY TIME IT IS HARD IS WHEN YOU ARE SAYING A FINAL GOODBYE TO SOMEONE WHO MEANS MORE TO YOU THAN ANYTHING:

I'll always love you!

WORDS WILL SEEM TRITE AND YOU'LL FOREVER REGRET YOUR INABILITY TO EXPRESS YOURSELF. THE END!

i have long held that t2 is the platonic form of action movies. all it's missing is a sex scene, and all that does to a movie is make it awkward to watch with your parents, so whatever! living liquid metal robots from the future NEVA4GET

HEY T-REX

TODAY IS THE DAY WHEN EVERYONE HAS TO TELL A STORY FROM THEIR PAST BEGINNING WITH "I WAS WALKING DOWN THE STREET TOPLESS"

Denied!

TODAY is the day we talk about meritocracy!

In a meritocracy all jobs, including government jobs, are assigned based on MERIT. So if you're the best at a job then it's yours, regardless of your sex or gender or race or stupid mustachio or anything!

But what if I'm awesome at set design while also truly despising all aspects of set design?

Then you wouldn't actually be the best! You'd get some other job you're better at. The result: PURE UNCUT UTOPIA.

Yeah, the only problem is there's absolutely no way to accurately judge merit!

Sure there is!

No way dude! You'd have to know the exact skills AND future potential of EVERYONE. If you had some omniscient and impartial third party then MAYBE, but you'll never get rid of cronyism when you have regular dudes trying to determine who's best. There's too much potential for authoritarianism and corruption!

God! Can YOU be an omniscient and impartial third party for me?

HEY YOU KNOW WHAT WOULD HAVE BEEN BETTER THAN TALKING ABOUT MERITOCRACY

TOPLESS

FRIGGIN

FRIENDS

if you randomly typed in 'qwantz.com' to your browser looking for topless friends, then boy! you are partially in luck!

mulvey LATER wrote that the paper in which she talked about the male gaze was meant more as 'provocation' than 'well-reasoned argument'. sweet! this is a great way to silence critics. this is the 'hah - you fell for it suckers!' school of debate. the only allowable response is 'oh man, you got me! you got me!!'

'too much poo' is the result of trying not to offend delicate sensibilities with the word 'diarrhoea', but then coming up with a euphemism that is more emphatic than the word it's trying to replace. if you life is like mine, then there are hundreds more similar examples in your past! that's crazy!

i may just have to sit down and write "Dudes! Lesbians! Guess what? Here is How to Get Women to Like You'.
it is a great title for a book because it appeals to both dudes AND lesbians.

c-can you tell them that - that t-rex sent you?

i sit really quietly, and when they try to talk to me i play 'in the hall of the mountain king' on a synthesizer that only synthesizes the screams of children

863

this comic is based on a story where i was talking with a guy and the guy said 'ryan you sure do use a lot of exclamation marks' and i said 'we're talking! how can you tell if i'm using them or not?' and hold on wait this story's no good

determinism: seriously guys, let's never talk about it again!

an orbital tower is a elevator that goes straight up into SPACE. i believe that it is the first time that it has been suggested that one could jump out of them onto giant trampolines. arthur c clarke called satellites but i call this!

"THE TALENT SHOW"

Dromiceiomimus, I have a great idea for our act: let's put on a play!

A Batman play!

A Batman play? What's a Batman play?

It's a play about BATMAN! I'll play Batman!

Sorry T-Rex! NOT INTERESTED.

My friend, nobody wants to put on a "Batman play"!

But I'LL be playing Batman!

How is that a selling point? If we were to put on a Batman play, we'd probably all want to play Batman. That is the essential folly of the Batman play.

Okay FINE, we'll do Plan Omega. Upon closer inspection, I can see myself REALLY getting into Plan Omega!

PLAN OMEGA:
Hi we're T-Rex and Utahraptor and we'll be performing "Push It" by Salt-N-Pepa in the original French.

Cette danse n'est pas pour tout le monde, c'est SEULEMENT pour les personnes sexuelles.

Poussez-le bon!

Poussez-le VRAIMENT bon!

my birthday wish it to have dinosaurs sing 80s hip hop in bad french! you probably have similar desires

So there's this guy I know, and he must be a friend of a friend because I see him sometimes at parties, but WE can never be friends because I find looking at him intensely frustrating. He has the world's most punchable face!

T-REX AND THE GUY WITH THE WORLD'S MOST PUNCHABLE FACE

And it's terrible! It reflects poorly on me, I know, but there's just something about him that is BAD for me. It's like being sexually attracted in reverse? I just end up avoiding the guy. He's got a stupid face for jerks!

sigh

I guess I just can't get past my prejudice against people with stupid faces for jerks.

Oh man, I knew a guy like that!

Really?

Yeah! We went to the same school. He's the only guy I've ever felt that way about!

I know! It's the same with me. MY ONLY CONSOLATION is that somebody else probably thinks I, T-Rex, have a stupid face, so at least I'll get my prejudice from both sides.

A FEW WEEKS LATER:

Hey you! You've got a stupid face! I- I want to punch it!

This somehow validates my own prejudice, mysterious stranger across the street!

I get that a lot!!

you can use 'sexually attracted in reverse' to describe all sorts of things you don't like! like for example, a mcdonalds fish sandwich is like sexual attraction in reverse.

869

In the past I have called my fists "Knuckles and Chuckles", and then later upgraded to the truly compelling "Rocco and Choco, the Twins! Who! Punch!" but now I have an even better nickname!

The CHINESE BUFFET!

That way I can menace someone with my fists and say "Do you WANT to visit the Chinese Buffet? It's all you can eat TONIGHT, baby!"

All you can eat?

All you can eat KNUCKLE SANDWICHES! The Chinese Buffet serves Chinese food AND knuckle sandwiches to those who are cruisin' for a steaming plate of them. I cannot stress this enough: it's all you can eat.

I can ALSO say "Looks like it's LADIES' NIGHT at the Buffet tonight!" Hee hee!

For when you... beat up women?

No, for after I beat up a dude and want to imply that he's actually a woman, in case he's the sort of guy who gets mad at that! Although I COULD also use it if I fought women - like, a cabal of sexy, yet EVIL, librarians!

You will be prepared if that happens! The only problem is: you're not Chinese?

LATER:
God! Can you make me Chinese so that my fist nickname makes sense?

ONLY IF YOU PROMISE TO PUNCH A GUY INTO THE OCEAN AND SAY AT THE BUFFET WATER IS ON THE HOUSE

Oh that is so a deal.

you'd think a dude with such good and practiced stomping skills would focus more on his feet than his fists, but sometimes all we can focus on is our weak points. THAT IS SOME DEEP AND MEANINGFUL STUFF THERE DUDES AND LADIES

if there was a superhero with a time-reversing ray then i guess you could call him Time-Reversing Ray

872 t-rex how could superman possibly know his own birthday? his parents put him in a rocket ship when he was a baby. that's crazy!

if you're looking to set yourself up for a fall, you should go around telling people how to intend to remain sane. then if you go crazy later on, oh wow! everyone will say 'remember how intent he used to be on remaining sane? how ironic.'

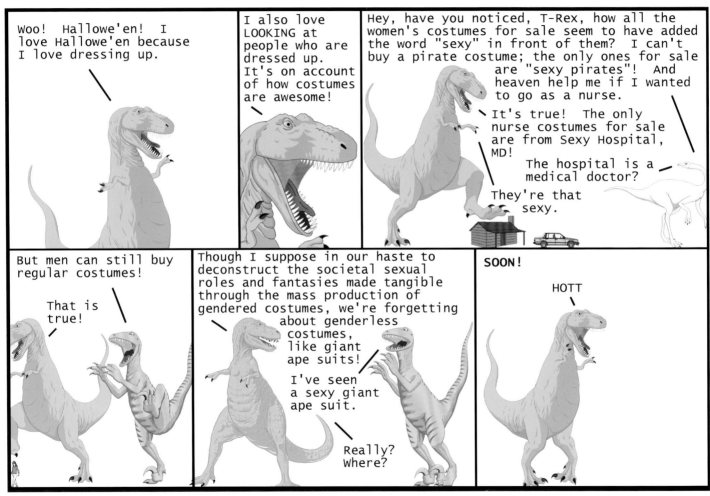

Woo! Hallowe'en! I love Hallowe'en because I love dressing up.

I also love LOOKING at people who are dressed up. It's on account of how costumes are awesome!

Hey, have you noticed, T-Rex, how all the women's costumes for sale seem to have added the word "sexy" in front of them? I can't buy a pirate costume; the only ones for sale are "sexy pirates"! And heaven help me if I wanted to go as a nurse.

It's true! The only nurse costumes for sale are from Sexy Hospital, MD!

The hospital is a medical doctor?

They're that sexy.

But men can still buy regular costumes!

That is true!

Though I suppose in our haste to deconstruct the societal sexual roles and fantasies made tangible through the mass production of gendered costumes, we're forgetting about genderless costumes, like giant ape suits!

I've seen a sexy giant ape suit.

Really? Where?

SOON!

HOTT

874   remember, t-rex's costume this year is the uncanny valley! he had to make the costume himself because at the store all they had was sexy uncanny valley.

if you're struggling with big questions like ''why am i here?'', consider: it may be because a dinosaur, just before the cretaceous-tertiary extinction event, wanted a joke to be real.

Who here would like to hear an old joke about oatmeal?

DAAAMN

I WOULD

Then here we go!

Okay okay, so there's this monastery, with three monks, and only one monk is allowed to speak, once, each year. They take turns! The first year, at breakfast, the first monk speaks and says "I hate oatmeal." A year later, again at breakfast, the second monk speaks and says "I love oatmeal." Finally, one year later, the last monk gets to speak and HE says "I'm tired of this constant bickering about oatmeal!"

Hee hee! Comedy gold!

Aw, that's an old joke!

BUT A GOOD ONE! It's funny, I think, because the conversation is spread over three years, and NORMALLY, you'd expect monks not to talk about oatmeal for that long.

I think it's funny because monks are normally thought of as holy, not as oatmeal obsessed OR oatmeal loathing!

I THINK IT'S FUNNY BECAUSE IT'S BASED ON A TRUE STORY

Is it?

WELL NO BUT I CAN MAKE IT SO IT IS IF YOU WANT

Dude!!

I'm afraid I'll have to insist!

876   if i can steal a joke from drmcninja.com: if you didn't whisper to yourself 'i do!' in the first panel, then either you have heard a lot of old jokes about oatmeal, or you are lying.

ATTENTION AUTHORS: please to write more books where the narrator rates the ending's satifiability in the last line of each story. are we cool

T-REX HAS SNUCK INTO UTAHRAPTOR'S HOUSE AND SWITCHED THE HOT AND COLD PIPES LEADING TO HIS BATHROOM SINK.

Tee hee!

LET'S WATCH!

Isn't that kind of an expensive, elaborate prank, T-Rex? The worst that'll happen is he'll get cold water when he expects hot.

Hilarious!

Maybe he'll burn himself a little!

COMEDY RELENTLESSLY ENSUES??

Hey T-Rex! What's new?

Hey Utahraptor! How's your bathroom sink treating you?

Oh, same old, same old! "The good ol' bathroom sink", you know? Good ol' reliable whitey!

Huh!

Well! I guess I'm not a qualified plumber after all!

BUT, THREE PLUMBING DEGREES LATER!

Hey Utahraptor! How's your bathroom sink treating you?

Whitey's hot and cold pipes got reversed!

Awesome, man! Awesome!!

yeah, utahraptor calls his bathroom sink whitey. people sometimes call for his sink to be killed?

The Problem with Wikipedia is that it's peppered with vandalism at various times and at various locations: vandalism that remains until it's noticed by someone who knows enough and cares enough to fix it! SOMETIMES THIS CAN TAKE A WHILE But!

ahem

Ladies and gentlemen: I have solved the Wikipedia Problem!

The solution is as brilliant as it is awesome: instead of vandalizing the ENTIRE encyclopedia, we all just agree to vandalize one article, leaving the other ones alone! That article is the one about chickens. Why? It's pretty obvious. DUDES ALREADY KNOW ABOUT CHICKENS.

In conceding that one TINY article to the vandals, Wikipedia wins! Their victory: a FULLY ACCURATE encyclopledia that covers every topic in the universe, 'cept chickens.

T-Rex, this is worse than taking on the mob! Wikipedia will be HELLUVA mad at you!

No way! I am doing them a FAVOUR.

Their vandalism problem GOES AWAY, FOREVER, and all that I ask is that chickens become The Forbidden Topic. "We never talk about chickens", they can say. "DON'T ASK."

But how are you going to get people to respect this idea? Plus, IS IT NOT TRUE THAT MANY WIKIPEDIA EDITORS ARE TRULY HUMOURLESS ABOUT WIKIPEDIA??

I guess we're about to find out! I bet Fictional Jimbo Wales love the idea.

I do love this idea, T-Rex!

Fictional Jimbo Wales! You brought cupcakes!!

fictional jimbo wales, you old charmer! PS: I KINDA WROTE A MANIFESTO ABOUT THIS, IT IS AT EVERYTOPICINTHEUNIVERSEEXCEPTCHICKENS.COM

879

can you just call utahraptor and, you know, casually mention that you would though? i PROMISE that there'll be no consequences.
i PROMISE.

you could go over to Invention Personified's house and her mother would serve you all these super tasty cookies and you could say 'You've made some very delicious cookies, Mrs. Personified' and she'd say 'oh, please, call me Necessity!' AND HEY PRESTO THAT IS A LOT OF BACKSTORY FOR A PUN

yes! be that guy who beings leprechauns to the table

Literally hours of work have paid off, and I have come up with my greatest invention yet... a DUPLICATOR RAY!

(Duplicator rays let you make perfect copies of anything!)

Really? So if I have, say, a papier-mâché piñata dog filled with tasty candies, your duplicator ray will make a PERFECT duplicate?

Yep! The duplicate is identical in every regard. The ray examines the object at the quantum AND subquantum levels and thanks to the twin fists of Actual Science and Heisenberg Compensators, makes a perfect copy, indistinguishable from the original!

I call baloney, T-Rex! Aha! On account of how it violates conservation of energy laws?

Nope, on account of how it's truly impossible to have a perfect copy of anything! Philosophically: if I paint a picture and you duplicate it, I'll grant that they can be identical in every way BUT ONE: mine is the original. That's a property that doesn't have a physical realization, so you can't ever duplicate it!

Okay YEAH it's not original, but it's an OTHERWISE PERFECT DUPLICATE. I can destroy economies based on scarcity and generate clean drinking water for everyone! I can even DUPLICATE DUDES! I can't believe you're not more excited.

I CAN DUPLICATE BRENT SPINER

he played 'data' on star trek. it's an exciting prospect, having your own brent spiner.

883

884

A negative income tax, or "NIT", is when the government pays you money when your income is low! Pretty sweet!

NEGATIVE INCOME TAX COMICS

it will be interesting I PROMISE

But there is a catch. You still pay taxes – say, a flat tax of 10% – BUT, the government also pays you enough to survive! This way there's a guaranteed minimum income – like welfare, but simpler. So if you make only $1000 in a year you'll pay $100 in taxes, but since the government pays everyone, say, $10000, you'll end up $9900 ahead in tax money, As you make more money, you net less from the government, until you end up actually paying taxes!

So this acts to replace welfare?

Yep! And a bunch of related pro-grams.

It simplifies things, plus it includes a flat tax, which a lot of amateur economists AS WELL AS even some real economists like!

I can see fraud being a problem, though, especially since if the fraud's successful, the govern-ment loses real money.

LATER:
Utahraptor! I just found out that Milton Friedman, proposer of the NIT, died yesterday at age 94!

One wonders if our conversation today would be an appropriate epitaph.

Dude! I believe this not to be the case!!

you can point all your happily married friends to this comic and say 'see? you may have found someone to share your life with, but *i* get to read comics on the internet'. wait

886

if you're about to marry someone, ask yourself: do i love this person enough to not party with jodie foster EVER AGAIN? if so, you should tell them that! they'd love to hear it!

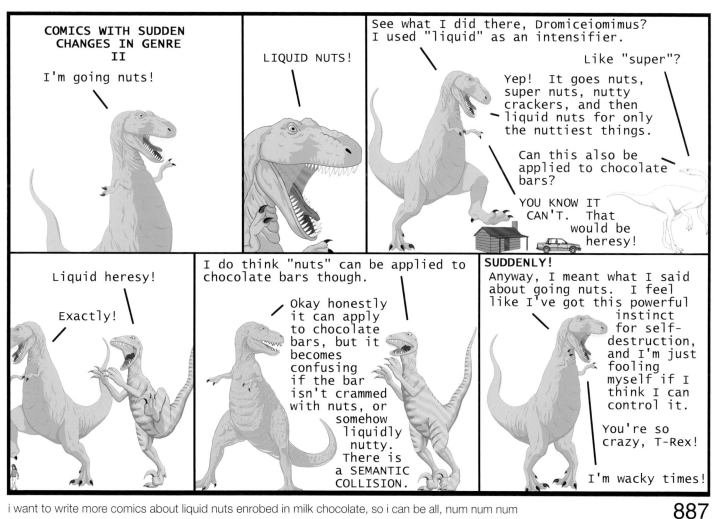

COMICS WITH SUDDEN CHANGES IN GENRE II

I'm going nuts!

LIQUID NUTS!

See what I did there, Dromiceiomimus? I used "liquid" as an intensifier.

Like "super"?

Yep! It goes nuts, super nuts, nutty crackers, and then liquid nuts for only the nuttiest things.

Can this also be applied to chocolate bars?

YOU KNOW IT CAN'T. That would be heresy!

Liquid heresy!

Exactly!

I do think "nuts" can be applied to chocolate bars though.

Okay honestly it can apply to chocolate bars, but it becomes confusing if the bar isn't crammed with nuts, or somehow liquidly nutty. There is a SEMANTIC COLLISION.

SUDDENLY!

Anyway, I meant what I said about going nuts. I feel like I've got this powerful instinct for self-destruction, and I'm just fooling myself if I think I can control it.

You're so crazy, T-Rex!

I'm wacky times!

i want to write more comics about liquid nuts enrobed in milk chocolate, so i can be all, num num num

they're not actually sure if they need his torso or not, but it's best not to take chances with the Widowmaker

later: instead of writing an opera, t-rex writes to an elected official complaining about how he can't write an opera. he rationalizes to himself that they are pretty much the same thing, then goes to bed.

next time you do the dishes, ask yourself if the dishes are clean, or if they're PHYSICAL INTIMACY clean. you may want to aim for the latter!

891

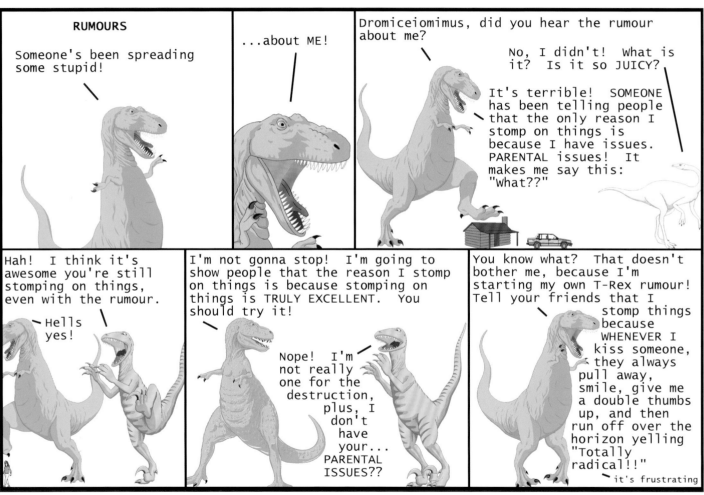

RUMOURS

Someone's been spreading some stupid!

...about ME!

Dromiceiomimus, did you hear the rumour about me?

No, I didn't! What is it? Is it so JUICY?

It's terrible! SOMEONE has been telling people that the only reason I stomp on things is because I have issues. PARENTAL issues! It makes me say this: "What??"

Hah! I think it's awesome you're still stomping on things, even with the rumour.

Hells yes!

I'm not gonna stop! I'm going to show people that the reason I stomp on things is because stomping on things is TRULY EXCELLENT. You should try it!

Nope! I'm not really one for the destruction, plus, I don't have your... PARENTAL ISSUES??

You know what? That doesn't bother me, because I'm starting my own T-Rex rumour! Tell your friends that I stomp things because WHENEVER I kiss someone, they always pull away, smile, give me a double thumbs up, and then run off over the horizon yelling "Totally radical!!"

it's frustrating

it's the midas touch for double thumbs up and unbridled pro-kissing pan-horizon enthusiasm

It's time to spice things up, dudes and ladies! Today I am only going to make BAD DECISIONS.

BAD DECISIONS COMICS

Aw no, T-Rex! Why can't you be like a regular person and only make bad decisions by mistake? I don't get this romance you have for regret.

It's exciting, Dromiceiomimus! And I guess I do like the IDEA of bad decisions more than I like the, you know, ACTUAL CONSEQUENCES of bad decisions, but this might cure me of that at least!

So let's hear these bad decisions then!

I haven't made any yet!

The only idea I have right now is to invent kitchen appliances that somehow crave the flesh of the living. That'd be a bad decision, right?

Kinda?

EXCELLENT.

SOON:

Don't try to eat me, toaster!

i won't t-rex

I can see you licking your lips while looking at my sumptuous belly, toaster!

awww darn

this comic is probably not fair to buddhism because i understand the scientific method a lot better than i understand the steps to enlightenment. if you're enlightened, um, please let me know?

t-rex has a point, they do make movies out of perfect storms

please, sir, come in! take off your jaunty chapeau and vest and have some tea, and we'll talk about this partying!

897

why do people with controversial theories about emigration always feel the need to volunteer their controversial theories about emigration? riddle me THAT

this comic is based on a time when i accidentally almost walked over a tiny woman at the airport. she was like three feet tall! it was truly impossible to see her

while trying to write the title text for this comic i said out loud 'i need some title text!', and my brother yelled 'that's not all you need!' from his room. ouch! what the hell, victor?

Congealed Human Suffering, it is the worst thing for a sitcom to be

901

902   the Nobel Oscar Prize is given out each year to someone who makes an outstanding contribution to humanity by being super good at movies, but it can't be a movie about mathematics. it's a - it's a confusing prize? and i think its origin has something to do with a review being prematurely published about a movie being dynamite?

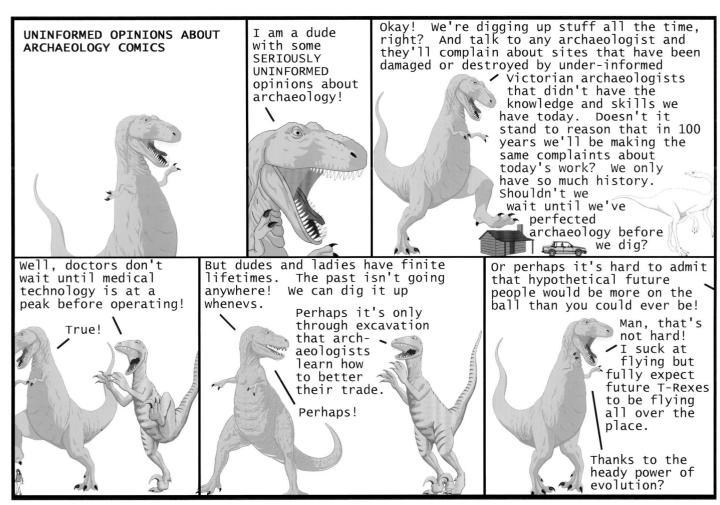

UNINFORMED OPINIONS ABOUT ARCHAEOLOGY COMICS

I am a dude with some SERIOUSLY UNINFORMED opinions about archaeology!

Okay! We're digging up stuff all the time, right? And talk to any archaeologist and they'll complain about sites that have been damaged or destroyed by under-informed Victorian archaeologists that didn't have the knowledge and skills we have today. Doesn't it stand to reason that in 100 years we'll be making the same complaints about today's work? We only have so much history. Shouldn't we wait until we've perfected archaeology before we dig?

Well, doctors don't wait until medical technology is at a peak before operating!

True!

But dudes and ladies have finite lifetimes. The past isn't going anywhere! We can dig it up whenevs.

Perhaps it's only through excavation that arch-aeologists learn how to better their trade.

Perhaps!

Or perhaps it's hard to admit that hypothetical future people would be more on the ball than you could ever be!

Man, that's not hard! I suck at flying but fully expect future T-Rexes to be flying all over the place.

Thanks to the heady power of evolution?

he's not talking about birds. he's talking about full sized t-rexes who can fly. i am not one to say that evolution dropped the ball here, but i know one consonant-loving former nasa roboticist who would be living in ABJECT TERROR today if there were flying velociraptors roaming the skies!

INFORMED OPINIONS ABOUT ARCHAEOLOGY COMICS

Yes! I have actually done some research this time. Schwing!

And it turns out I was TOTALLY CORRECT!

Archaeologists ARE aware that they're mining a finite resource, and when possible, they only dig a little and leave some for the future. But there are time limits: often they'll be examining a site just before it's dug up for a new building or something, which means this is their last chance to see what's there before it's destroyed. And sometimes the ground is volatile enough that if they don't dig soon, whatever's there will be lost anyway!

In conclusion and in summary, way to go archaeologists!

Hooray for archaeologists!

We have nothing but good things to say about the women and men of archaeology! Nothing but smiles for the trained and capable few who dedicate themselves towards exploring and explaining our shared history!

LATER: ARCHAEOLOGISTS TOTAL T-REX'S CAR!

Damn it, archaeologists!

oh, archaeologists, you were doing so well

aw t-rex, it's not a failed relationship! relationships aren't cockfighting: they're not a failure if they don't last until one or both of the participants are dead!

alternate ending: god says 'T-REX SOMEONE HAS ALREADY OPENED A STORE CALLED THE RELATIONSHOP' and t-rex yells to utahraptor that God says the idea is already taken, but that they're going back in time to prevent the idea from being preemptively stolen, and god's all 'I NEVER SAID THAT BUT DAAAMN LET'S GO BACK IN FRIGGIN' TIME' and then they all meet marty mcfly

if you are personally insolvent, it is a good idea to inform the dudes

he totally was!!

Someone going by the all-caps name "ZACH MORRIS" has tagged my house! My front door is now spraypainted with "Zach"'s stupid name for jerks. I don't even like Saved By The Bell that much!

Forget you, Zach Morris!

I thought you liked street art, T-Rex! You're always all "Hey guys, let's reclaim public spaces with art instead of ads".

Yeah, but this isn't art! It's tagging. It's just some dude's made up name! Taggers are like dogs, marking their territory wherever they can, and "Zach Morris" is just a dog who likes implausible high school scenarios. Either that, I guess, or Mark-Paul Gosselaar is bored. And experimenting?

I think you're ignoring the symbolism AND sociology behind tagging, T-Rex!

Explain!

Okay, so you grow up in the city, and the skyline is dominated by billboards, ads for products and brands you don't have access to. And you realize that nobody cares who you are, but EVERYONE knows who Mickey Mouse is and what a Coke is. So you create a brand for yourself! You make up a tag and put it everywhere.

Tagging can really be seen as the logical next step in ads: self-advertising! It can be seen as the price we pay for a culture that has saturated itself with advertising: individual brands, internalized campaigns of self-promotion.

UTAHRAPTOR YOU ARE ZACH MORRIS

908

all of dinosaur comics has been building to t-rex saying "forget you, zach morris!" in panel two. FACT

there is some debate over the spelling of 'zach morris' in yesterday's comic. some say it should be spelled 'zack', while others maintain that bad spelling is a proud tagging tradition! if you're reading through the comics backwards, then dude! guess what! zach morris is in the next comic!

Index Alpha: Suggested Email Subject Lines

for when you need to write to me about what you have just read

723 a tip of the hat to all our brave men and women who have swallowed a lot of orange juice for no reason

724 LB-BFF bracelets

725 ryan, i have heard that the chinese word for 'crisis' is the same as the english word for 'opportunity', can this possibly be true

726 dromiceiomimus is wrong, people were probably named 'pine' in the sixties. i don't know. it seems plausible, doesn't it? i heard there was a lot of 'crazy stuff' going on in the sixties.

727 dromiceiomimus is the best at tellin' regrets. she's not actually that regretful, she just tells the regrets she has SO WELL.

728 hey ryan more facts about this genital massage treatment please

729 t-rex has been reading up on producer slang, and you can tell because of how he uses the word 'talent'.

730 the popcorn didn't get burnt or anything, he just forgot about it and now it's all cold

731 t-rex could just takes frost's 'stopping by woods on a snowy evening', replace 'evening' with 'morning' and 'woods' to 'traffic intersection' and then feel terrible about himself.

732 ryan you can have a wacky adventure on a planned cruise dromi is right and you should acknowledge this

733 it's like saying 'aunt flo' is visiting, only instead you hollah that mc masturbation is in the HOUSE

734 DID YOU KNOW that twincest is not in the microsoft word 2003 dictionary, as shipped? come on, microsoft word 2003 dictionary! my fanfic has enough red underlines as it is.

735 it's true that music with words can have a narrative, but who ever cried over fastball's 'the way'? NOT ME. ONLY A LITTLE.

736 RYAN IT IS ACTUALLY EXACTLY THE OPPOSITE WHAT ARE YOU DOING????

737 t-rex is taking the 'door-to-door bible salesman' approach to selling books, which in my experience is where you call everyone 'friend' and talk about all the good news you're privy to.

738 t-rex's opinion is that if you change the past, you shouldn't be surprised at how sucky a time traveller you are.

739 there's no reason to say 'astonishing' anymore. you can use 'bistonishing' in every single situation where 'astonishing' might apply.

740 t-rex is mentioning needing to be bailed out of jail pretty often, should we be concerned ryan

741 so yeah, he's not a guy you can reliably take to indian restaurants

742 this comic went up a little late ryan, probably because it took you like an hour to get the thought bubble right.

743 ryan, the thought bubble was so nice you used it twice

744 are there porn magazines called 'topless lesbian teens'? it seems almost too straightforward.

745 i am britishfolk and 'nappy' means 'diaper' to me, so this comic is very confusing and maybe a little perverted.

746 it is probably best to avoid using the phrase "sexual predator" when describing yourself! I KNOW THIS NOW

747 woo! shouts out to Arthur's Medical Clipart!

748 MY QUERY IS WHETHER OR NOT BETA TESTING POSITIONS ARE YET AVAILABLE

749 meanwhile, in a universe absolutely constrained by its premise!

750 panel six raises a lot of questions and my only choice is to declare it SO NON-CANON

751 the only meal t-rex can still really believe in is breakfast

752 forget work! let's go to the beach to hang out in flattering swimsuits!

753 the first time - the first time was an accident.

754 a poor little puppy with an injured leg, pulling a mobile iv behind, one squeaky wheel announcing him wherever he goes

755 was dromiceiomimus going to invite him too, but never got a chance to get a word in edgewise? we may never know.

756 man, looks like SOMEONE was trying to register 'quartz.com' three years ago and decided to make the best of it

757 being stranded on the moon is a serious Problem

758 when i come down from a speed run i like to rub my face on the carpet, cool

759 see, because he's been stomping on people for so long, thereby violating their rights! CONTINUITY

760 the dystopian future clearly stems from a war between dinosaurs and tiny women

761 IF THIS BE MY DESTINY...!

762 man, t-rex has clearly learnt his ABCs (always be selling / closing)

763 oh slap happy t-rex, how could i ever stay mad at you

764 ryan can you do a comic about the song 'two princes' by 'spin doctors'? it's good and it's stuck in my head right now! 'just go ahead now' is what they sing

765 that's right, 'memorable love-making techniqueS'. it's plural now.

766 endless hunger for the flesh of the living? shit, no!

767 as a pet duck owner i get this ALL THE TIME

768 a lot of things suddenly make sense

769 the caps in panel 4 make the ENDLESS BATTLE FOR SURVIVAL seem EVEN MORE EXTREME!!!

770 at the end, t-rex is fine with people who talk about true love, but not those who are focused on finding 'the one'. he has learnt more about himself. it has truly been A Day For The Diary.

771 i'm so tough that when i think about feelings all i do is punch friggin' cement walls

772 ryan, did - did poor little morris ever make it home?

773 apparently t-rex has used the 'hot chicks were on their way but, you know, car troubles' excuse on utahraptor before! i can see that

774 wait, i'm a brilliant email composer!

775 i'm fading away, i'm sick of this life, i just wanna scream, how could this bad thing be probable to happen to meeeeeee

776 gray also invented an early fax machine called 'the tel-autograph', which serves to remind us of how, since the 1950s, we've all SERIOUSLY dropped the ball when it comes to naming machines

777 is utahraptor's favourite song really 'all the things she said' by tatu? it is an easy guess to make because secretly that is everyone's favourite song.

778 you take the cruise ship and put it in your pocket. ouch!

779 utahraptor probably named his bike after the aimee mann song, and not that loveable a softer world character, 'handjob susan'

780 this one goes out to the extreme mother with baby carriage i saw, may the MAN at toronto city hall one day stop getting all up in your fries

781 each and every day humour struggles to keep up with you, ryan

782 ryan i like how you took pains to define cockfighting for those of us who are unfamiliar with, um, blood sports.

783 t-rex is a dude entirely for citrus. have you had lemonade? it's nuts!

784 x-men 3: regret index .99992 :(

785 utahraptor's moral was you should never let your cat eat gross stuff off the ground.

786 i'd much rather spend my time in the french rap universe D:

787 SOME of them.

788 it is a common mistake to assume that those who visit dentists have bad oral hygiene. this is not necessarily the case! many visit dentists as part of a regular 'check up' regime in order to ensure that their GOOD oral hygiene is maintained. if you believe that all those who visit dentists don't brush their teeth very well, then yours is the face of prejudice.

789 and then the dude's mind breaks?

790 one of t-rex's fundamental beliefs is that you can find a way to kiss someone so hard you both explode. with great power comes great responsibility, etc

791 i would also have accepted 't-rex has an ape / let's see what happens'

792 pansandwichism is the belief that everything, the entire universe, is literally sandwiches

793 ryan you forgot to include bank managers (usually not so sexy, but there are notable exceptions) and surfers (kind of sexy, but what if they're bank managers when they're not surfing? it's too risky.)

794 man forget you ryan giving away all our manly secrets and so on

795 what's the deal, logs? what's the loggy deal?

796 man, there are some rough chuckles here against stupid guys nobody likes, RYAN

797 HoverPants are pants that hover for some reason. they exist, but the government doesn't want you to own them, man!

798 the narrator suggests to the subject that she is a gold digger by way of roman irony

799 this one goes out to all the brothers and mothers who, unknowingly, begin today an endless series of very bad decisions

800 utahraptor is wrong: incurable stealie-o-holicism is a real affliction. there are ads on buses for it, but incurable stealie-o-hols keep stealin 'em

801 the feeling i get when i put both my fists into my mouth is an exact, identifiable, reproducible joy that i can only label 'mouth ouchies'

802 MAYBE INDIA WILL SOLVE MY PERSONAL PROBLEMS

803 RYAN i live in an area where the age of majority is not 18, so i'm mentally changing the age in the first panel to make it more appropriate. okay, awesome

804 the old saying of 'when in doubt whip it out' does not apply to feelings! just weiners!

805 the high five is the rarely-seen but oft-rumoured 'four-way' high five

806 dinosaur comics, featuring Off-Panel Poe

807 if you've eaten cheetos and you're not a hobo, WELL THEN, you're doing it wrong

808 you may be able to stop me, officer, but can you stop my fleet of specially trained ESCAPE HELICOPTERS???

809 if your eyes are a chartreusey shade of puce, then LOOK AGAIN, because man they're not

810 RYAN WE NEED TO TALK ABOUT PREGNANCY IN DINOSAURS OKAY

811 this is like when someone asks you to guess what they had for dinner, and you say something like 'a watermelon with a sauce', and they look at you funny, and you realize you have revealed TOO MUCH

812 later: everybody dies and then eats the brains of the living, while also handily serving as a powerful image of the conformity of society!

813 VISUAL ARTISTS: if you want to convert a real gun to fire caps 19 times out of 20 but a real bullet that twentieth time, and then paint it to look like a toy gun, i'm PRETTY SURE some art juries would find that to be

a pretty powerful statement on something (childhood? gun violence? i leave the choice up to you) and you could get your 'piece' into galleries.

814 facial hair dudes don't just have facial hair, they make having facial hair a very important part of WHO THEY ARE. facial hair dudes got their own problems

815 t-rex clarifies what he loves about punch in the first panel, in case punchophiles in the audience get the wrong idea

816 man evil is such a useful term huh

817 for a much more depressing comic, replace 'thirsty' with 'lonely' in the last panel.

818 quick! to the abandoned violin factory!

819 but RYAN my name is ben and i jam rarely if ever

820 ryan has your obsession with littering, revenge, and poo bugs finally gone too far

821 ryan how did you know i love delicious sandwiches?

822 the canonical example is 'are you still beating your wife', not 'are you still punching children'. why are you trying to whitewash wifebeating and tacitly endorsing the endemic punching of our nation's youth?

823 that or he could examine the sources of his dissatisfaction and look for things that could re-energize his daily routine but yeah let's try solving this problem with make outs first

824 there's actually a special heaven for people who have said things that had never been said before. it is called, 'unpopular phrasing heaven'.

825 utahraptor's being a little hard on t-rex, but on the other hand, he didn't build a robot suit

826 dude uses his analogies to OPINE and EDUCATE

827 MY narrative of life features scenes of adult content. parental discretion is advised!

828 dude is one of the gloried few suggestible enough to rise to the rank of captain!

829 asperger's syndrome: the syndrome everyone on the internet wants to have?

830 you got me, ryan! i do lend god money!

831 RYAN STOP STEALING MY BOOK IDEAS! DANGGGG

832 yes, inspiration can come from anywhere, even divorce!!

833 the sign for driving a car is pretty much exactly what you might expect

834 utahraptor had trouble seeing the benefit in marrying a beautiful and wonderful woman! it's because he's gay or whatever!

835 t-rex should ACTUALLY be saying 'everyone i ever kissed in high school is awesome' but i think it's fair to assume that the trend continued up to the present day.

836 my breakfast pleasure is a glass of juice, some oatmeal, and some fish-oil pills

837 awwwwwww snapadoodle!!

838 lie serum is available in either big transparent containers or teeeeny tiny little white ones

839 have i made my 'sexual congress is now in session' joke before? if not, sexual congress is now in session

840 are these 'menergies' truly the result of combining raw men with raw energy?

841 gentlemen! here is a dating tip! never call anyone a 'potential lifemate'!

842 two comics in as many days mentioning poops i thought we were CLASSY around here RYAN

843 god is playing devil's advocate!

844 thanks ryan or should I say thanks CHUANG TZU OF THE 4TH CENTURY BCE

845 i could seriously marry a librarian, no sweat

846 i use 'thanks for the helpful TERRORISM TIPS'. it leads to hilarious circumstances for people other than myself!

847 you can call me 'the dude with the compellingly graphic haircut'

848 the idea of the uncanny valley is credited to masahiro mori, a japanese roboticist! he came up with it in the 70s. a lot of robots were pretty freaky in the 70s, so yeah!

849 the REAL question here is why the ladies don't go wild for my heavy-ass skull

850 DREADED CONTINUITY! also: it's been kind a big week for t-rex meeting new people. also: why go on a road trip to the island continent of australia, when it's closer to drive a car straight into outer space?

851 why must you tease me with the word dude in only a mere 66 percent of all panels?? i demand 100 percent satisfaction!

852 did you get your inspiration for the place where owls rule the world like they don't even care from this place i made up, where owls rule the world like they don't even care

853 beards over babies might well be eclipsed by its sister typo organization, bears over babies

854 memory contents will be wiped off after you leave, so tell me about your problems

855 making itself intelligible is suicide for philosophy

856 mine is this endless black and white loop of an old rick ety bike at night, slowly driving itself down a rain-soaked road

857 if i could talk to t-rex i would say, hello t-rex, what are your thoughts on 'friends with benefits' because check out these benefits

858 WHAT WAS THAT ABOUT MY STUPID MUSTACHIO

859 i wrote my own comic wherein this man stares lecherously at his mail and the caption says 'the mail gaze'. HA HA MONEY PLZ

860 it is a running joke at my house that if you are wearing a shirt with a number on it, then that number is the number of problems you have. we saw a dude who had more problems than gretzky

861 the full version of chapter 3 should have a 'wow!' after the 'intercourse ensues!'.

862 t-rex is super impressed with the speed at which off-panel heterosexual chicks and gay dudes operate. i am too, honestly!

863 man, fuck you guys! i'm going in the boat!

864 it's like if you block a pipe in a cartoon, the exclamation marks form a big bulge and then come spilling out every where

865 im in ur base, sexin ur d00ds

866 for extra determinism, loop back a big crunch to the big bang, and you've got an endless looping movie of pre-determined reality

867 you land, high fives, a final kiss, and kapow! PROBLEM SOLVED

868 why would you call something 'plan b' when you could call it 'plan omega'? i ask you

869 guys i'm sexually attracted in reverse so hard to ben af-fleck right now

870 sexy librarians i am on to you

871 i wanna to be a dick tracy villain, mr half babyface

872 oh, my drinkey shame

873 instead of richard iii, it'll be richard ii! wait.

874 for this comic to make sense, you have to imagine that there's someone in a sexy giant ape suit, and that their current location is always known to utahraptor. THIS IS REASONABLE

875 RYAN I HAVE LEARNT SO MUCH ABOUT UTAHRAP-TORS TODAY

876 But the monks, sitting lonely eating oatmeal there, spoke only / Of the oatmeal, as if their souls in that one theme they did outpour

877 DUDE last night i accidentally ate too many candy corns by mistake D:

878 it's how t-rex knows the most recent plumbing degree actually took. in plumbing circles, they call that a 'trial by water'. no they don't, don't listen to me

879 whenever you talk about wikipedia here at dinosaur comics, fictional jimbo wales shows up. it is a 'tradition', in that it's a tradition for him to INVITE HIS INVENTIVE ASS OVER

880 i like my dates like i like my women: surprising and memorable

881 science and religion both calling shotgun: a powerful metaphor for our times?

882 ryan, i... i liked it when you called me 'baby' in panel two

883 hold up your preferrered fist in front of you as you say 'the twin fists of Actual Science', and then bring the other parallel to the first as you say 'and Heisenberg Compensators'

884 hip hip

885 ryan are you trying to stir things up again because on my messageboard of choice we argue about flat taxes all the time, and i'm all like, whoah

886 i love jodie foster. i think she's great.

887 THAT genre didn't last very long

888 i think it's kind of funny that utahraptor came running when he heard about a 'new sexual position'. not THAT funny, but, you know - kind of funny.

889 'mammalian breast' is like 'male prostate', in that the adjective is there just to underline the fact that you're paid by the word

890 how are the ol' emotions

891 ryan more comics about your female friends and their naughty adventures PLEASE

892 fight fire with even stupider, yet more flattering, fire

893 ryan i expect more bad decisions from t-rex, how about tomorrow he can take out library books and then not return them and then, i don't know, you're the writer here

894 the first version of this comic that went up had a typo where instead of betting t-rex fifty bucks that *he* can't achieve enlightenment, god dropped the 'you' and instead said 'HEY T-REX I BET YOU FIFTY BUCKS CAN'T ACHIEVE ENLIGHTENMENT', which made the whole comic hella more surreal

895 can photoshops make t-rex with mittens though

896 attentive readers will notice how t-rex uses two homophones in his speech in panel 3, which would be really confusing if you're weren't reading it as text. luckily, dromiceiomimus is blessed with the uncanny ability to distinguish between homophones! it's an ability that doesn't come up much, but she's fine with that. it's useful when it does, and that's all that matters.

897 you know in back to the future ii, where marty's out in the rain and this guy shows up out of NOWHERE with a message for him, sent from the year 1885? wait, that wasn't a telegram, NEVERMIND

898 they - they make dictionaries in braille, t-rex, if that would affect your decision

899 how about lending me your clothes? no dice? what a drag!

900 i miss her emergency pauses for self-narration :(

901 ryan more timely comics about sitcoms years after they went off the air please

902 have i ever seen someone use an emoticon in speech, and what's more, add an exclamation mark to it? I HAVE NOW

903 utah phillips would say that archaeological sites are a natural resource, and would go on to ask if you've seen what they do to natural resources.

904 i just found out that 'totalled' comes from the car insurance industry, where a car is declared 'totalled' if its total repair costs are greater than the price of just buying a new one! neat

905 number three in the "use the 'email this comic to a friend' feature of the website to cause Problems in your social life" series

906 in an abusive relationshop and the staff is SO RUDE

907 ryan if you die today your last comic will have a punchline about poo so KEEP THAT IN MIND WHILE SKYDIVING or computer programming or whatever

908 ryan please start a new comic called ''Mark-Paul Gosse-laar is Bored and Experimenting" i would read that SO HARD

909 utahraptor is accepting the wishes of good luck at face value. it's maybe not that bad an idea!

Index Beta: Context-Free Punchlines

Index Omega: An Actual Index For You to Use

An interview with ME

Here's excerpts from an interview I did with Karen Whaley of Torontoist.com, sometime in the middle of these comics being written. Karen and I met in a restaurant where we chatted and ate before she turned on the microphone and did the interview for real. It was a great technique – we'd already gotten the "I just met you so let's both be awkward!" times out of the way and the interview was better for it.

You are a computational linguist by trade, but you're also a webcartoonist. Does being a webcartoonist take up most of your time?

Actually, when I graduated I started doing the comics full-time and didn't tell anyone but my friends, because I was worried that if I missed a day people would be like, "What the hell? You're not doing anything else, what's the deal?" So that was fine, but I had this problem where I'd get up, start writing the comic at 7:00, finish it by 9:00 or 10:00, do a bit more stuff, and at about 2:00 every day I'd start getting really bored because I had nothing to do. It was like Spring Break for about a week, but then you're like, "Oh my God, I'm wasting my life!"

So I started doing more programming: I made a webcomic search engine called OhNoRobot.com and recently, a site for RSS feeds called RSSpect.com. It's really sweet because I can do the comic in the morning, which I love, and then spend the afternoon on personal projects, which I also love. I'm a full-time webcartoonist, but I'm also a programmer – that is, if you're allowed to be full-time and still cultivate something else!

I've heard from people that the way T-Rex talks and the things he speaks about are very similar to you, and that Dinosaur Comics is sort of autobiographical in a way. So, I guess the question is, is it even possible for you to run out of material?

Well, this is the problem, because sometimes I do autobiographical stuff where I'll lift things from conversations I've had or things that have happened to me. But then sometimes I don't! There was one time last year where a newspaper on campus published a comic about T-Rex having sex with two women at the same time and I haven't done that. People were congratulating me, "Ryan, way to go! You da man, cool guy!" and I was like, "Uhh...I...I just made that up". I'm actually sadder for having imagined it.

Dinosaur Comics in unique in the sense that it has a fixed structure. Is it easier to fit what you want to say into a repetitive frame system?

When I started the comic, I did sixteen all at once. I was worried that the structure would be too restricting because you have these dinosaurs and there's a narrative implied in their motions. But what I quickly realized was that you could do stuff like say that one panel is taking place three weeks later, or "Meanwhile in an alternate universe..." So you can always toy with narration to change the fixed structure, which gives you a lot of flexibility.

I feel like I was insanely lucky when I made that template. The way the characters are framed adds a beat to it. Like the first panel is the introduction, the second panel you have to do something there that's suggestive of the conversation, the third panel is another angle. So it really supports a conversational narrative, which is cool because I didn't expect it.

As the comic's protagonist, T-Rex is obviously the most popular character. Tell us a bit about Dromeceiomimus and Utahraptor, who don't necessarily get the same attention.

Dromeceiomimus is a smaller, female dinosaur. Actually, she was originally male, but I wrote a comic that needed a woman in it so she became female. Apparently everything is male by default in my worldview? Dromeceiomimus is sensible and cute and tolerant. Utahraptor is more questioning and interrogative; he and T-Rex have more of a back-and-forth wordplay between them. They don't insult each other, but...

It's funny, T-Rex is the most popular dinosaur but Dromeceiomimus, it turns out, is the fastest whereas Utahraptor is probably the smartest with the largest brain-to-body mass ratio, so they're three very unique dinosaurs.

Is there an underlying romantic storyline between T-Rex and Dromeceiomimus?

T-Rex and Dromeceiomimus dated for a while, and they're still sort of quasi-dating in that I haven't really specified whether it's just maybe something on the side. Utahraptor maintains that he and T-Rex had a homosexual affair – though I've never talked to any gay people who call them homosexual affairs – in the bath and T-Rex can't remember it.

So let's say they turn Dinosaur Comics into a feature film and you're brought in to cast the movie. Who plays whom?

Oh, easy. I would cast based on actors I like. So you'd have Patrick Stewart as T-Rex, and for Dromeciomimus...hmm, I can't think of any female actors. Brent Spiner as Utahraptor and...Michael Dorn as Dromeceiomimus?

So essentially _Dinosaur Comics: The Movie_ will be a big episode of

A photo of Michael Dorn I found on Wikipedia.

Star Trek: The Next Generation!

Exactly, and they're all men. And God would be played by LeVar Burton and the Devil by Wil Wheaton.

So would Michael Dorn be in drag?

Oh, absolutely! I assume that he'd turn up to the casting call in full drag.

You were recently involved in the arrest of some 15-year-old girls in Ravenna, Ohio. What happened?

A friend of mine who goes by the name "Posterchild", because some of what he does is technically illegal, made these three cubes and painted them so they looked like the question blocks from _Mario Bros._ and put them up in Windsor. The politics behind it was that public spaces can be grey and uniform, especially

Question block photo by Posterchild

in a town like Windsor. Why is it that you can put up an advertisement in a park or street, but you can't put art there? His idea was that instead of putting art in a gallery, he'd put art in the streets. People react and respond to it: you get the public engaged in their environment. I put up a website a year ago with instructions, and people made their own blocks all over the States, Australia and the U.K. I found one in Toronto, it's up in my living room right now.

On April first this year, these girls in Ravenna made some boxes and people who saw them called the police. The anti-terrorism squad got called in to defuse them, as if they were bombs.

[Karen and Ryan snicker]

I shouldn't laugh. I ended up updating the site, warning that if you don't know what the Mario Brothers are, a big box with a question mark on it might seem like a bomb. From what I heard, the Mayor of Ravenna was pissed that they had wasted the bomb squad's time and money and wanted to find a way to make the girls pay for it. They were trying to find something they could charge the girls with and throw them in jail, but they couldn't because there wasn't a law prohibiting it. Since the press was watching the story, the town said that they wouldn't charge the girls if they wrote a letter of apology to every law enforcement agency involved saying that they wouldn't do it again. The girls said they were making T-shirts for themselves and some teachers that had been supportive with a question block on the front and the phrase "NOT A BOMB" written on the back.

When the story broke, I started getting four to five e-mails a minute. The story ended up getting reported on all the major cultural websites, and I even got an e-mail from Jack Thompson, the video game crusader, who called ME a jerk.

So what's it like being Internet Famous?

It's weird having more readers. It started with just me, my mom and my friend Mel reading it. Now there's 70,000 people a day looking at the site, and you have a louder voice that people react to. Being Internet Famous is alright: you can just turn it off by going outside where nobody knows who you are and think "Okay, I'm really not that great, I'm just a guy who has a website". So if you want to be famous, go for Internet Famous. If you want to get a big head, go online, and if you want to feel normal, go outside.

Last but not least: summarize your entire being in one or two sentences.

Ryan North is an awesome dude, period. Also, handsome. No wait: Ryan North is awesome, comma, oh-so handsome.

Can you do that in a haiku?

Yeah! 5-7-5? *[long silence]* No, I can't.

Ryan North wrote these comics; he lives in Toronto. He got a degree in computers at Carleton University, then he got a degree in computational linguistics at the University of Toronto. Then he graduated and became an internet cartoonist on account of how it's the best job in the world! Later on, Emily Horne took this photo of him.

You can read more of his comics online every day at qwantz.com! PROBABLY, you already knew this?

TOPATOCO™

THE WORLD'S MOST FLAMMABLE COMICS

PROBLEM SLEUTH
by **Andrew Hussie**

This is a book that is also a game. It is about a detective who can't get out of his office! You play the game as you read the book. You tell the detective what to do, and he does it. He breaks his desk, and finds candy corn in his pocket. And more!

books: **topatoco.com/mspa**
read online: **mspaintadventures.com**

NEVER LEARN ANYTHING FROM HISTORY

HARK! A VAGRANT
by **Kate Beaton**

Remember when history was boring? Too many facts, man, that's the problem. Let's get rid of some of those, and put some better ones in! Let's add some more stories about fat ponies and Tom Cruise, even better. Perfect.

books: **topatoco.com/vagrant**
read online: **harkavagrant.com**

OVERCOMPENSATING
by **Jeffrey J. Rowland**

Overcompensating is the almost 100% true journal comic of cowboy-poet/hacker/CEO/amateur electrician Jeffrey Rowland, who happens to harbor a seething disdain for reality. There is a person in it called Weedmaster P and a green cat that is maybe a zombie.

books: **topatoco.com/wigu**
read online: **overcompensating.com**

WONDERMARK
by **David Malki !**

A sarcastic, silly, and razor-sharp gag comic strip created entirely from 19th-Century woodcuts, this Eisner-, Harvey-, and Ignatz-nominated comic is in equal measures strange, attractive, clever and good-natured—*just like you.*

books: **topatoco.com/wondermark**
read online: **wondermark.com**

A SOFTER WORLD
by **Joey Comeau & Emily Horne**

A Softer World comics are like a weird sad clown that lives under your bed. Except the tears are blood. And when the clown coughs, the most adorable kitten in the world pops out of his mouth and loves you.

books: **topatoco.com/asofterworld**
read online: **asofterworld.com**

THE ADVENTURES OF DR. McNINJA
by **Christopher Hastings**

He's the doctor who cured Paul Bunyan's Disease, the disease that turns you into a giant lumberjack. He's the ninja who defeated the raptor-riding Mexican bandits, and gained a mustachioed 12-year-old sidekick in the process. He's a man who encounters an above-average amount of explosions. He's Dr. McNinja.

books: **topatoco.com/raptorbandit**
read online: **drmcninja.com**